The Map

of

Mind

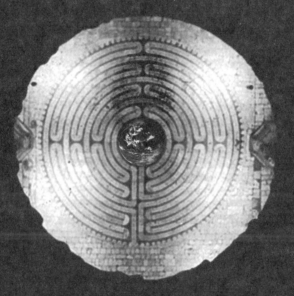

An Explorer's Guide to the
Labyrinth of the Mind

Master Djwhal Khul
through Kathlyn Kingdon

The Matter of Mind

Master Djwhal Khul through
Kathlyn Kingdon

Light Technology Publishing

ISBN-10   1-891824-63-5
ISBN-13   978-1891824630

Published by

3ॐLIGHT
Technology
PUBLISHING

800-450-0985
www.lighttechnology.com

PO Box 3540
Flagstaff, AZ 86003

About Kathlyn Kingdon

Kathlyn L. Kingdon, MA—board-certified clinical hypnotherapist and cofounder of Madison Street Counseling Center, Women's Mysteries Tours, the Rocky Mountain Enneagram Center and The Vajra Flame Foundation, Ltd.—is a true renaissance woman. Her lifetime achievements hold distinction in multiple professional fields.

An experienced conference presenter, she has designed programs for corporate and educational entities to assist with organizational change and employee empowerment. She has offered workshops on group process, grief work, optimal human functioning and the sacred feminine. She has also lectured on the use of music and voice to enhance personal functioning at physical, emotional, mental and spiritual levels, and has recorded and published several instructional CDs used by Dynamic Listening Systems of Denver, Colorado, and their providers. Additionally, she served as editor for the psychological publication, *The Journal of Giftedness and Gifted Education*, published by the Gifted Development Center in Denver, Colorado.

Kingdon was the keynote speaker at the International Goddess Conference in Glastonbury, England in 1997, lecturing both on Dion Fortune, renowned British kabbalist, and the feminine force in traditional Hopi kachinas. She was keynote presenter at the International Summit of World Healers held in Monterey, California, in 1998, and was also featured at the International Conflict Resolution Conference, held in St. Petersburg, Russia, in 1999, where she introduced the Enneagram as a viable tool for conflict resolution. Additionally, from 1988 to 1999, she led tours and presented to groups of women in the field of Women's Spirituality in Ireland, England, Wales, Scotland, France and India. Perhaps her most significant contributions, however, lie in the meditation retreats and channeled workshops she has led in some fifteen of the United States as well as abroad.

Kathlyn's career path is broad and varied, owing to what she terms her "short attention span." The fact that she holds a compelling interest in nearly all facets of life is demonstrated in her work in the world.

She was the first woman to graduate from Colorado University with her master's degree work completed in conducting. She then taught school in Colorado at both the high school and middle school level—teaching not only music, but also science and drama at the middle school level, writing and directing four children's plays during her two-year term.

Kathlyn then became fascinated with graphic arts, so she left teaching and over the next six years set up three graphic-design businesses. First she opened a commercial camera center (The Lens), offering local offset printers and screen printers a complete range of photographic services. Next came a printing supply company (Pueblo Printing and Litho Supply), and later a complete graphic arts center was added (La Graphiques Excalibre).

From graphic arts, Kathlyn moved into law firm administration, working for one of the large 17th Street law firms in Denver. Then, having taxed her left-brain significantly in the legal world, Kathlyn returned to school, taking immersion courses and special educational programs by leaders in the field of transpersonal psychology, specializing in optimal human functioning and neo-Reichian work. Additionally, she became a certified Enneagram instructor and meditation teacher. During this time, she also traveled coast to coast as a spiritual channel and in 1992 formed a tour company dedicated to discovering high-energy and sacred places around the world.

As a writer, Kathlyn has authored numerous articles in various fields of interest, ranging from Christian education and the problems of legalism in religion (in the 1970s); to reviews of complicated law cases, nutrition and paper consumption (in the 1980s); to the effects of quantum physics on the field of psychotherapy, the place of the sacred feminine in psychotherapy and personal development, and the feminine life cycle as a spiritual path (in the 1990s). Additionally, she published a collection of provocative poems, *Poems to Ponder upon the Path*, in 1987, as well as a year-long personal journaling experience, *Journey into Softness—A Reflective Experience Designed to Help Loosen Hard Edges*, in 1997. She also wrote the film script for *A Spiritual Pilgrimage to France* in 1996.

A trained professional singer and voice trainer, until recently Kathlyn maintained a small studio of voice students. Her high point as a conductor came in 1983, when she was one of several conductors to participate in the Denver Symphony Orchestra's fiftieth anniversary celebration, which was taped for PBS release that same year.

Born in southern California but raised in a small farming community on the South Dakota prairies, even as a child Kathlyn had a wonderful fascination for life's mysteries, great and small. Her profound love for and connection to nature has been a source of inspiration and fulfillment since early childhood, earning her the reputation as a "bee charmer" at age five. Kathlyn's earliest visitations from nonphysical teachers came at age three, and she received direct communication and training on a daily basis until age six. At that time, she was instructed to place her focus in the external world, to discover the rigors of the physical plane and seek accomplishment therein.

Raised in the paradigm of strict fundamentalist Christianity, Kathlyn began exploring past lives through hypnosis with her friends in college. Her curiosity about world religions was then piqued, becoming an area of deep exploration for her over the years. In 1983, at the age of thirty-six, she was introduced to Master Djwhal Khul through personal circumstances that led her to the voice channel Janet McClure. In her first interview with Master "D.K.," as he is sometimes affectionately called, he opened to her the path he said she had chosen before incarnating in this life—that of the voice channel.

Although her primary commitment has been to Master Djwhal Khul all these years, when asked to provide a conduit through whom other spiritual masters can teach, she has willingly obliged them as well. Her body-mind space has been opened to numerous great ones, including a specifically dedicated three-year commitment to Vywamus and a four-year commitment to Modron. When asked to comment on her adventures with these great teachers, Kathlyn, in her often understated way, reflected: "It hasn't been boring!"

Known affectionately as "the Tibetan," Ascended Master Djwhal Khul is one of the planetary Wisdom Masters, well known to spiritual aspirants the world over. A master teacher in every respect, he imparts timeless truths from many spiritual traditions in contemporary terms, and graces all his beloved students with his loving wisdom, sincere compassion, and profound generosity. The depth of his priceless teachings challenges the mind and touches the soul.

Table of Contents

An Introduction i
   The Four Bodies and the Mind i
   The Path to Union: The Real Work of a Spiritual Journey iii
   My Current Mission Is to Aid Humanity
      in Actualizing Enlightenment v

Mind as Tyrant 1
   Perception and Experience 1
   The World as You See It Comes from *Your* Creative Process 3
   An Old Taoist Tale 6
   A Barrage of Projections Are Defining Who You Are 7
   Your Liberation Is Completely in Your Hands 9
   Engaging the Heart 11
   Pay Attention to Your Projections 13
   Find Your Buddha Within 16

Mind as Creator 19
   Narcissism Is Very Seductive 19
   Narcissism and Spirituality 21
   The Image Mask Is But an Imitation of the True Self 24
   Artificial Connections with Others 27
   Waking Up from Your Mind Trance 28
   Getting to Genuine Authenticity 31
   Love Is Your Essential Nature 32

How Karma Works 35
   Initial Thought and Developing Thought 35
   Don't Confuse the Karma with the Person 37
   Westerners Are in a Most Auspicious
      Life for Working through Karma 39
   Karma Also Manifests through the Body 41
   Mastering Karma Requires Challenging Your Own Mind 42

The Long Road to Freedom 44
As Karma Dissolves, Purification Practices Become Important ... 46
Every Piece of Karma Is *Just a Thought*! 47
A Visualization for Mind Renewal 48

Karma and the Mind 51

The Play of Karma and Emptiness 52
The Value of Direct Experience 54
Enlightenment Already Exists in Your Essence Mind 55
Essence Mind vs. Ego Mind in Relationships 57
Shifting from the "I/Me" to the "We" 60
Learning to Look through the Eyes of Essence 61
The Potential of Essence Activating Essence 63
Clarity Is a Gift of Emptiness 64

How Karma Ripens 67

The Ripening of Karma 68
The Power of Perception 69
The Influence of Collective Perceptions 71
Fullness vs. Emptiness in Western Society 73
How One Gets Stuck in the Past 74
The Workings of Karma Are Deeply Hidden 76
Seek to Be in Charge of Your Mind 78
The Thief and the Monastery: A Gift of Radical Awakening 80

Mind as Liberator 83

Learning to Look through the Eyes of Essence 84
Karma and Your Death 85
Dissolving Karmic Projections 86
Discovering Oneself beyond Ego Boundaries 88
To Know Liberation, One Must Have the Experience 90
Your World Is a Creation of Your Mind 93

Working with the Mind 95

The Naming of *Samsara* 96
The First Energetic Field: Altruistic Thought 97
The Second Energy Field: All-Embracing Compassion 99

Transcendent Wisdom: The Third Energetic Field 101
Practice Generating These Energies 104

From Emotional Reactivity to Enlightenment 107

Arjuna and Gandhi, and the Call to Duty 107
Duty Is the Vehicle to Liberation 110
Negotiating the Emotional Terrain 112
Waking Up to Your Natural State 116
The Value of Direct Experience 117

Assembling the Puzzle 121

Humans on Earth and the Domination Mindset 121
The Diamond Net of Indra 123
The Rise of Reductionism and the Scientific Method 124
The First Proposition:
    Human Development Has Reached Its Pinnacle 125
The Three Rungs of the Space Continuum 127
The Three Corresponding Rungs on the
    Time/Consciousness Continuum 129
The Second Proposition: Each Thing Is Separate 133
The Third Proposition: Physical Reality Is All That Exists 134
When Contemplative Mind Awakens to the Miracle of Life 136
Moving Beyond the Tenets of Conventional Science 139

Death and the Mind 141

Experiencing the Death Process 142
The Transition through the Tunnel 143
Undergoing the Life Review Process 145
The Stupor Phase 146
The Journey of the *Bardo* 148
Preparing for the *Bardo* Journey 151
The Awareness Is Released for Rebirth 154
Stay Awake! 155

Where Is the Mind? 159

Exploring the Placement of Mind 159
Mind Awareness after Death 161

Facing the *Bardo* 163
Learn to Tame the Mind 164
Be the Radiant Glory You Were Meant to Be 165

An Introduction

My beloved students, I greet you in the majesty of divine consciousness, and I celebrate with you the beauty of your becoming. Know that your life is very precious, for it offers you the opportunity to open to your true nature. What a wonder is the vehicle you know as your body-mind, for it allows you to experience and learn from substance, form, structure, movement, perception, integration, appreciation and, above all, the cocreative process of spiritualizing matter. Celebrate the journey, and dedicate everything you learn to the liberation of all beings everywhere!

This book is a study of the mind. Part of the material is taken from public lectures I have given through Kathlyn Kingdon in our twenty-something-year partnership. Those recorded lectures are available through the Vajra Flame Foundation, Ltd. [www.vajraflame.org]. This book is not merely a collection of lecture transcriptions but of teachings that utilize some of the same material found in those lectures with additional commentary addressed to a larger student audience. You will notice that the fluff has been removed, with each sentence being as direct and forthright as possible. It is my earnest desire that spiritual students everywhere will find within these pages informative principles that will aid each in negotiating the interesting, if complicated, terrain of the mind.

The Four Bodies and the Mind

The word "mind," as I use it in this text, should be interpreted broadly and should be seen to include all four bodies. The *physical body* is the seat of the organs of perception, which are experienced through the five senses. The *emotional body* presents the wide range of the feeling spectrum that so permeates the life of the human being. The *mental body* is the source of cognition, conceptualization, analysis, interpretation, discernment and judgment, to name a few of the functions. The *spiritual body*—an emanation from the Source of All Being—is an oceanic flow of pure consciousness that contains the field of infinite possibilities.

Receiving information from the other three bodies, the spiritual body remains divinely neutral and is both the supreme integrator of truth and the dispenser of wisdom. The spiritual body anchors into human awareness as the internal quiet but perpetual observer. The spiritual body contains the other three bodies but vibrates at a much higher frequency than any one of the other three or combination of those three. It is therefore not limited by the conventions of time and space, and in highly evolved individuals, it extends outward from one's physical point on the planet into deep space, holding the very formula for creation.

Individually, each of these four bodies provides a complicated array of awareness factors. Collectively, they present a spectrum of awareness possibilities so vast that the average person can scarcely be said to do more than scratch the surface on this massive expanse of terrain called mind. In this text, for the sake of simplifying a very complex landscape, I make continual references to *ego mind*, which draws predominantly from the lower three bodies, and *essence mind*, which draws predominantly from the spiritual body. Other terminology is used to identify specific attributes of mind—such as "hungry mind," "distracted mind" or "doubting mind"—that are seen as emanating from ego mind.

Suggestions given for working with the mind or training the mind tend to be activities that engage the mental body. The material with which one works or trains, however, arises predominantly from the emotional body. Thus can be seen the interdependent relationship that exists between these two as they continually offer input to the flow of consciousness. Although the physical body is addressed much less directly in this work, its presence in all exercises of mind must be implied, since the physical body houses the organs of perception, the neuronal system and the convoluted mass of gray and white tissue that fills the cranium—the brain.

The Path to Union: The Real Work of a Spiritual Journey

This study is not intended to contradict the teachings of any spiritual tradition, although it assumes certain spiritual notions that are not universally accepted by spiritual aspirants of all spiritual traditions. Cyclic existence, for example, appears as a given in this text. Although roughly 90 percent of the world's population believe or at least accept reincarnation as a viable spiritual tenet, another 10 percent reject its viability. Of course, these world figures are not generally reflected in Western religions. Even though there is a growing openness to this notion in the West, those of a more fundamentalist persuasion—this applies to certain segments of Christianity, Judaism and Islam—may only view it as little more than a vehicle for excusing dysfunctional behavior. For example, the phrase, "The devil made me do it," may simply be changed to, "My karma made me do it." Even if one sees a modicum of truth present in these remarks, still, both these statements reveal a level of spiritual immaturity that must be transcended.

The proposition of cyclic existence is really no more problematic for the logical mind than something like a virgin birth or perhaps resurrection from death. For the most part, one accepts the doctrines and belief systems that have been normalized by the culture in which one is raised. Rather than trying to determine the absolute certainty of particular spiritual tenets or doctrine, it is a more workable situation spiritually to simply allow for the possibility that truth sometimes hides within mystery. In this way, one avoids going down the slippery slope of resistance and doubt. Indeed, many possibilities are always abundantly present, and you will likely discover that as possibilities are encountered, they may be described in remarkably different parameters person to person. For example, the notion of cyclic existence might seem self-evident to one but completely impossible to another. In the end, both may discover that there are limitations to the notions they hold sacred.

This text should not be viewed as a vehicle to convert individuals from one belief structure to another. Rather, it is intended to stretch the minds of those who grapple with its material, opening them to a greater field of possibilities than was present before the reading. It is my wish that this collection of teachings might serve as an adjunct to all teachings that advocate taming and/or transcending the mind. This text is neither a clinical text nor a psychological text, although it may be seen as an adjunct to both. Its purpose is to guide the serious spiritual student in negotiating the less-obvious operations of mind and can be utilized by proponents of all spiritual paths.

Although this text may not be the last word on the mind, it should at the very least provide readers with a basic understanding of not only how the mind creates but also how karmic patterns arise again and again under the auspices of the mind. Indeed, at less spiritually evolved levels of awareness, it is difficult to distinguish between karma and mind, since the two are so deeply intertwined. With the elevation of that awareness, however, insight arises as to the nature of both karma and mind.

Less lengthy than some of my prior works through other channels, this text is a straightforward and uncomplicated presentation of material that I feel is basic to all spiritual growth. In my extensive work with Western students, I have noticed that in the quest for comprehension of the universe, often the basic practices that provide the path to liberation are either overlooked or neglected. Many Westerners are afflicted with the belief that if they could just understand the universe, there would be no need to sustain a spiritual practice. It is believed that having such a great understanding would liberate their minds from the repetitive tendency toward suffering. The belief that there is some great truth out there that will bestow the gift of liberation on all who find it is unfortunately somewhat like the belief in Santa Claus.

Entertaining vast concepts is interesting and engaging to the mind, and can be instructional at a number of levels. No matter how significantly the mental body may be stretched, however, such will never offer a replacement for the cultivation of basic goodness and genuine concern for all sentient beings. Many people feel that they are, in fact, basically good and therefore have no need to further cultivate that goodness. Likewise, most people hold some philosophical concern for other beings but might not see the need to further cultivate that concern. It is possible to conceive of oneself as basically good, even concerned for others, but still see oneself as somehow separate from all the suffering that arises for those "others." However, as goodness and loving concern for all beings is intentionally cultivated, the barriers that appear to divide self from other become more and more flimsy, until ultimately they completely dissolve.

The real work of a spiritual path is to discover what stands between oneself and the divine. The fact that the definition of the divine varies from tradition to tradition really matters very little. It is not the definition of the divine that blocks this union, for aspirants of all those traditions have discovered the path to union. Under rigorous investigation, it will always be discovered that it is the mind—or more specifically, how the mind moves in the interpretation of what it perceives—that stands between oneself and union with the divine.

My Current Mission Is to Aid Humanity in Actualizing Enlightenment

I would like to add a note for those of my students and others who have experienced my teachings primarily through Alice Bailey, which are printed and distributed by the Lucis Trust. I have noticed that those who first met me through the work with Alice either immediately recognize me or do not recognize me at all in my work through Kathlyn and other channels with whom I currently work. A common complaint by those who fail to recognize me is that the material I am currently generating does not appear of the same genre as the work through Alice. There is, of course, a reason for this.

Alice and I had a specific assignment, and that assignment was to put forth a range of resource material for humanity that would literally stretch the bounds of consciousness. The product of our considerable work was intended to expand the mental bodies of all who would study the material. Those teachings were put forth in the Western world at a time when few materials were available to Westerners that could encourage the expansion necessary to bring forth a New Age.

Although those teachings were never intended to take the place of science in the West, they were put forth in a style that captivated the scientific department of the mind. This style was specifically selected as a mode directed to the West, drawing salient principles from many spiritual traditions but expanding upon them in such a way as to stretch the parameters of the collective mind at the time. Clearly, a special channel was needed for the project. As to the purpose of our mission, Alice and I were both faithful and successful, and those volumes of loving effort grace many homes, organizations and libraries all over the world.

To those who are worried that I am not creating the same kind of material through channels at this time, the question must be posed as to why I would repeat the work I have completed through Alice. I stand by that work fully, and I have tremendous love and appreciation for the sacrifices Alice made to fulfill our commitment together.

As I previously mentioned, the work through Alice was created to expand the mental bodies of students around the world in preparation for a New Age. This was successfully accomplished, and my current mission is to aid humanity in actualizing enlightenment. What stands in the way of enlightenment for most is the residual karmic debris hidden away in the emotional body. I have seen that individuals can hold and understand great cosmic truths, yet they completely miss the less obvious workings of their own minds. Cosmic truths are expansive for the mind to entertain, but the real work of enlightenment is done as one faces the demons hiding in the emotional body.

Thus, I have returned once more as a teacher. I have neither the need nor the inclination to repeat the teachings I gave through Alice. Those writings were generated for the purpose given above and are still effectively stretching the minds of many around the world today. My current assignment is to aid humanity in opening to enlightenment, and this work is often done at such a personal level as to mandate one-on-one teachings, or teachings to small groups working on similar blocks. Through Janet McClure, I again entered the physical realm as a master teacher. It was through her dedication to my work that I was able to span greater physical distances and make contact with those who would work with me toward the end of the twentieth century and into the twenty-first.

I presently work through a number of channels, and the work I do through each is different in scope and intensity. I am deeply appreciative of the sacrifices each has made to facilitate the spiritual plane, particularly in the work of clearing the emotional body. My purpose in working through multiple channels is to reach all who will allow themselves to be drawn into vastness by the force of love and who, through their own endeavors, will further anchor the light potential of Earth in the conventional experience of the present moment.

I am deeply appreciative of the time, energy and dedication of Kathlyn in bringing through the work I have been able to do through her. Know that both she and I desire full liberation for each of you.

I am also deeply grateful to all the dedicated volunteers who have provided their time and energy in transcribing endless transcripts for the Vajra Flame Foundation, as well as to Diane Rasmussen for her contribution of endless hours of proofreading and error correction. Additionally, I am grateful for the dedicated work of the Vajra Flame Foundation's Board of Directors and various committees for taking over the many functions of my work that Kathlyn previously solely attended to. It has been the addition of the loving help and support of so many that has provided the time needed for Kathlyn to prepare this book.

Please join me and these who have contributed so much to this publication, that we might together celebrate the dawning of this New Age. This book is dedicated to the liberation of all sentient beings from all levels of suffering.

Mind as Tyrant

Whenever you find yourself living in a time that is riddled with chaotic and/or deceptive energy, you may notice that you feel rather small. When the confusion all around you is very large, what is one little psyche engulfed by all that confusion? You might ask yourself, "What can I do against all of this chaotic energy? What can any one person do?" Sometimes, as you perhaps know, there are no simple answers to the big questions. Often, if the answers seem too elusive and the energy overwhelming, one might collapse inward, feeling inadequate to face life. In that case, one may move into a stance of belligerence toward the world and perhaps walk around with the proverbial chip on the shoulder. Or one might become afraid and, as the saying goes, try to "jump in a hole and pull it in after you." In this latter case, one withdraws from the "reality" one perceives.

Some are able to face the appearance of chaos as a personal challenge and try to meet it creatively. We could, of course, continue to postulate a wide array of variations upon each of those themes, but perhaps what is really needed is a way to think outside the box. Let's consider stepping beyond the obvious altogether and viewing the big picture from a point above and beyond the experience you are having.

Perception and Experience

The way the body-mind normally works is through perception, which is based on sensation. The body is configured with five types of physical senses, and those senses are giving you an almost unimaginable amount of information virtually every moment. From this huge pool of information, the mind creates perceptions of the world around you. However, the process is somewhat deceptive, because instead of forming perceptions based on the sensations of the moment, the mind is actually cross-referencing the incoming perceptions with experiences from your past.

For instance, pretend for a moment you are a toddler sitting on the kitchen counter in a kitchen that is unfamiliar to you as your mother is talking with a friend. They are perhaps getting ready to make some tea, and she points out to you that you are sitting next to the stove. You have already learned that a "stove" can be "hot," but this stove doesn't look like what you know as "stove" at home. The one at home has coils on it that become red when hot, and you know by the redness not to touch them. This "stove," however, has pretty little blue flames dancing in a circle. The word "stove" doesn't compute with previous experiences of "stove." You study those pretty little blue flames, and mesmerized by the dance, you reach out to take one. Suddenly, your little hand is burned, and a functionally new understanding of "stove" becomes a part of your experiential stream.

Although this example is very simple, it does demonstrate the normal way in which one learns from his or her experiences. What really goes on in the body-mind involves tying whatever you think you perceive to what you've known in the past. Although this process seems pretty straightforward, it will eventually leave you with a problem: sooner or later, you quit observing your arising perceptions and merely relate to the world around you from your past experiences. Thus, the perception route is short-circuited by previous inferences and interpretations. Whenever you become familiar with something, you cease paying the kind of attention to it you paid before it became familiar to you.

Although the process itself is normal, like so many other parts of life, it has an upside and a downside. The upside is the ability to demonstrate that you have mastered some level of knowledge. The downside, however, is that you remove your attention. You see, but you don't *really* see. You hear, but you don't *really* hear. What you're really listening to and really looking at are the perceptions you have accumulated from your past experiences, which then get projected onto the experience of the moment.

Thus you end up not actually experiencing what is happening in the moment. You *believe* you are experiencing what is happening in the moment, but in truth, you are re-experiencing—or shall we say, re-creating—past experiences, complete with personal interpretations about those experiences. It is very interesting to observe the mind at work. If you study it carefully, you will find that it is both the agent that trips you up by confusing the present moment with the past and also the vehicle that opens the door to your freedom from suffering.

The key to finding the door to your freedom arises as you learn to transcend the mind. Until you learn to cut through the illusions of the mind, you will suffer under the mind's tyranny, for it is the mind's ability to project the past onto the present that causes suffering. The hard part here is that you have been conditioned to believe that you *are* your mind. This is the first basic illusion you must unravel. You must begin to ask yourself, "Who am I, if I am not my mind?" Of course, when you first begin to ask this question, you are asking only your mind. But as you continue the questioning, one day you will break through the parameters of mind and find your true nature, which is pure consciousness. Then the question becomes a door to profound discovery. No longer a cognitive process, the question becomes an invitation to the experience of your true nature.

The World as You See It Comes from *Your* Creative Process

Mind as you know it can work only through the process of projecting the past on to the slate of experiencing you think of as the present moment. Although those projections may have no reality of their own, they are in fact quite powerful. Never discount a projection simply because it is a projection. The ability of mind to project is no less powerful than some other state of awareness. If your mind projects a certain meaning about a specific experience, then for you in the moment, that is all that arises. Of course, as you grow spiritually, you will eventually come to see how deceptive the mind is with its habitual projecting. Eventually you realize that there is always more going on than the mind projects.

When you were young, you may remember being told that the Earth was round. At the time, you had no way to prove or disprove the proposition. You had no direct experience of seeing the whole Earth, so because everyone else seemed to believe that the Earth was round, you accepted it. There was, of course, a time when people believed that the Earth was flat, and they were as convinced about the rightness of that perspective as you are today about a different perspective. They, of course, told their children that the Earth was flat and that somewhere out on the horizon, they would fall off. Given this projection, it would only be logical for early maritime folk to conclude that they shouldn't stray too far from the land.

Enter Columbus. Although he was not the originator of the notion that the Earth's shape is spherical, he did at least raise the funds to back his adventure to substantiate the notion, irrespective of how hallucinogenic it must have seemed to the land dwellers of his own time. That notion of the Earth has served humanity quite well. It has allowed for the remarkable feat of navigating the globe by air, land and sea.

However, with the remarkable discoveries of quantum physics, today you are faced with new notions to define the Earth. Is it a solid chunk of mass orbiting the Sun in a fixed and predictable way, or is it a collection of infinite, mutable possibilities arising randomly in the field of the perceiver? There is, of course, a functional reality to perceiving the world as a sphere of solid mass, but is it the *real* reality? You could probably even make the case for the likelihood that notions of the world are products of mass hallucination—or at least mass projection.

Clearly, much of what you have accepted as true regarding the world around you has come from the projections (rightly or wrongly) of others. Often you have had no direct way of testing whether the assumptions held by the many are in fact true for you. Thus, for lack of a testing process, you just accept the assumptions and possibly pass them along to yet another generation. You accept the fact that when someone tells you they love (or hate) you, they actually do. Perhaps the real question is, "What is it that claims to love or to hate?" and "What is it that can be the object of projected love or hate?" Fortunately or unfortunately, you will always come back to the mind. The world as you see it comes from *your* creative process.

For instance, when you look at a group of people in a room, there appears to be a collection of individual beings, all separate from one another. You do not have any doubt as to where one of them ends and another begins. It does not appear that the group is really a single experience, nor that the entire Earth could possible be a single experience. Although the nature of the Earth experience is singular, the manner in which the experience is perceived is through millions and millions of filters—all those projected selves who are watching the experience and projecting their respective histories upon it. It is somewhat like putting on a pair of colored glasses and noting how the glasses change the way everything looks. For a little child, the *whole world* changes when he or she puts on those glasses. With a little age and experience, that same one realizes, "Oh, it's the glasses—the world stays the same."

Perhaps it is important to recognize that you are filtering every experience you undergo through the lens of your past experiences, whether from this life or others. Thus, as you look at the world and your own experiences, thinking perhaps that you understand them, be very careful with the perceptions you believe to be real. Notice when you feel a need to defend your "reality" to someone else. Notice those instances when you feel a need to argue with someone else's "reality" because yours seems more valid. Notice also how the mind will conveniently use every projected experience to its own advantage. Notice, and ask: "Who am I, if I am not my mind?"

In the process of generating your enlightenment, there will come a time when you will question virtually everything you have ever believed. As you begin to see through some of the mental constructs you merely accepted because there seemed no need to question them, the world as you previously knew it will begin to fall apart. In truth, it is not the world that falls apart but the mind that held the world in a certain way that begins to fall apart. As this happens, you begin to realize that your world arose and was reinforced by the ways in which you had seen it previously. All that held those notions together were movements of the mind, or karmic projections.

This is true even in your relationships with other people. As the mind crumbles, you realize that relationships too are mainly the result of projecting mind. You come to discover that most of what you think is a relationship to another person is in fact a relationship to your *notion* of the person. In relationships with those you see as terrific, you are projecting them as wonderful people. The same is true with those you deem less than wonderful. You see them through the lens of the projecting mind, and then you respond as if your projections are true!

The same mind, however, has been at work in every other corner of your created/projected reality as well. Suppose you arise one morning and you don't feel well. Based on the sensation you experience and the resulting perceptions that arise, you could project a negative aura upon your whole day. Unless you are very aware, you may think that what you perceive to be happening to you is coming from "out there." You see yourself as a victim of circumstance rather than as the one with the paintbrush who has colored the day in murky gray tones.

An Old Taoist Tale

Some of you doubtless know the old Taoist tale of the elderly Chinese men who always had tea together. One was older than the other three, so they came to his house every morning for tea. One day one of the three asked, "Old man, how go things for you? Is there any good news?" His reply was immediate: "Well, who can say? Who can say what is good or what is bad?" Another responded, "Tell us what happened since yesterday!" He replied, "Yesterday my son was working the horses and the gate broke, and they got out and ran away." The others said, "Oh, bad news! Bad fortune! Bad fortune!" But the old man's remarks were calm and quiet: "Well, who can say what is good or what is bad."

The following day they returned for tea, asking for news of the missing horses. The old man replied, "Well, the two horses that ran away came back last night, and they brought with them thirteen more wild horses. My son had repaired the corral, and now we have fifteen horses." To this the group shouted together, "Oh, good news! Good fortune, old man!" Thoughtfully, the old man replied, "Well, who can say what is good or what is bad."

The next day they came even earlier, inquiring of the recent events. The old man said, "My son was trying to break some of the wild horses and he fell off one and broke his ankle." In a chorus, the others chanted, "Oh, bad fortune! Bad fortune!" The old man, in his reflective way, simply replied, "Well, who can say what is good and what is bad."

The three village men came again the following morning asking how the old man's son was and whether there was any more news they should know about. The old man replied, "Well, after you left us yesterday, the army came around conscripting soldiers. My son didn't have to go because he had a broken ankle." "Ah! Good fortune! Good fortune!" the three intoned.

As you can see, the story could go on and on and on. What it offers, however, is a clear example of how the mind works. The three visiting men represent the mind, and as you can see from the story, after each day's news, the mind came up with a projection. There were, of course, the events of the day, and then there was the mental overlay, where the mind projected the events as either good or bad. In this story, real wisdom is held in the perspective of the old man, for his concern is not whether an event is good or bad but rather to clearly see *what is really going on!*

A Barrage of Projections Are Defining Who You Are

Appearances are very powerful, and if you are not carefully attending to your mind, they will fool you every time. You will never see your own Buddha nature or Christ nature if you cling to appearances. Those of you who are serious about your enlightenment must learn to see yourself in some way other than how you now appear to yourself. Some of you look in the mirror and count wrinkles. Then, with dismay, you act as if the image you perceived is who you really are. The tragedy, of course, is that as long as you believe such, you are forced to live it out. The creative mind is so powerful that it generates a projection and then *reads* the reflection as confirmation of the original projection.

Now, in truth, how everyone else sees you has something—indeed, *everything*—to do with your projecting mind. What you project about who you are becomes how the world sees you. You project an energy or aura, and those around you receive that projection, "reading" it in accordance with how they see you. Therefore, if you see yourself in some negative light, how can others avoid seeing you negatively? By the projections and perceptions of your mind, you give others the raw material for their perceptions of you. Others form their perceptions of you, which come back to you often on an unspoken energetic level. In one moment, they may see you with approval, but in another moment, the tables turn and they look upon you with disapproval. Whether you are conscious of this or not, you are receiving their projections about you, and you are taking them in, filtering them, denying them, reacting to them and so on.

Until you have seen through or transcended the mind, you cannot help but be subject to the barrage of projections regarding who you are. As we have seen, some come from you, and many come from others' observations of you. You could say that the energetic emanations you put out are your projections, whereas how people read those emanations are their projections. Clearly, your mind is not really separate from what you perceive to be the minds of others, for they are exchanging information all the time at subtle, unspoken levels. The problem is that neither your projections nor those of others are coming from the present moment. The mind can only work through a continual regurgitation of past perceptions and interpretations. This function can be called "movements of the mind" and are what you know as karma.

It is the power of karmic force that makes it so difficult for people to step out of the confines of the roles to which they have conformed. When a role or projected reality is "normalized," it is often exceedingly difficult for the mind to see that role as a projection, particularly if the role has been practiced for forty or fifty years. There is an old rural American saying that goes, "You can take the boy out of the country, but you can't take the country out of the boy."

By way of explanation, let's say a young man grew up on a farm, where as a child he was educated in a farming community and seen there by all his peers as just another farm boy. For the sake of our story, let's further say that he grows up, goes to college and graduates with a degree in an area quite removed from farming, perhaps in the arts. The young man recognizes he has a gift for acting and, leaving college, pursues an acting career. Perhaps he follows that path for a while, and like many actors, he finds that there are fewer and fewer opportunities to support himself in this career.

When the career starts to falter, often so too will the self-esteem. The young man may even come to believe he was not worthy of his own ambitions and dreams but should have stayed on the farm where he "belonged." Suddenly he finds that his own psyche simply will not let him have that which he was once capable of having. The projections of those who, back on the farm, saw him as just another farm kid again arise with new force. Ultimately, he will return to the farm—i.e., the familiar—perhaps even reclaiming the poor grammar and provincial colloquialisms he knew as a child.

You could say that our hypothetical young man never fulfilled his birth. Indeed, each is born to become whole, to take healing in the areas not yet healed from previous lives. If, however, one collapses under the collected projections of his or her childhood, the karmic force may simply overwhelm the possibilities for transformation. Although there are powerful examples of those who defy the odds, step into healing and flourish, such is not the normal pattern. Most will return to what is familiar, even in the face of great personal pain.

Because they are unaware of the mind's tyranny, most will re-create the irresolution from their past experiences again and again. It is as if the projections that one collects along life's way become a container of sorts, within which it seems safe to experience. Staying in the box, one takes no risks, ruffles no feathers. One simply lives with the projections of mind, as again and again the past is reinforced. Unfortunately, no transformation is available in the box.

Staying in the box, however, increases one's suffering. In fact, one will suffer and suffer until he or she simply *has* to get out of that box. Whether that escape is accomplished in the current life or a future life is likely to depend on how cramped one feels in the box. Eventually, the constant company of one's mental projections begins to feel suffocating, and within the psyche, a great crescendo of creative energy builds that may ultimately explode, propelling that one out of the box. To accomplish one's potential, one must learn to risk losing that familiar, if cramped, home in the box. From a spiritual perspective, the greater risk is in *not* breaking out, for what one stands to lose in that case is the set of wings with which one is destined to experience flight.

Your Liberation Is Completely in Your Hands

All have it within them to become Buddhas. Karma, of course, interrupts the movement into the potential self. Karma is commingled and perpetually interactive with mind. Thus, one must transcend or see through the mind in order to experience the true self. Karma and the mind reinforce each other in a powerful, if hidden, way. When one thinks he or she has seen through one of these, the other arises in deception, often through old, patterned ways of seeing self and the world. Ultimately, both must be transcended.

Most consider a Buddha or a Christ as someone or something "out there," a trick perpetuated by tyrannical mind. To become a Buddha or a Christ, one must learn to project oneself as a Buddha or a Christ. Clearly, this can be done only as the karmic projections are dissolved in the light of one's true nature. Of course, learning to project oneself differently starts in the mind. Although it is probably the most ardent task one will ever undertake, realizing enlightenment literally depends on "changing the mind" from holding limited projections to that of a Buddha.

In your personal journey, you will come to recognize that the matter of your liberation is completely in your own hands. Now, granted, all of creation is offering to help you by working very hard at reflecting your true nature in the beauty of the seasons, in the splendor of the night sky and by example of the bloom cycles of all the plants. However, it is ultimately up to you to see the true reflection instead of the countless limiting projections of the mind.

By way of example, imagine two people walking down a sidewalk that goes by a beautiful garden someone has lovingly created. The first person stops, for she cannot pass by without fully absorbing the beauty before her. She sees a magnificent creative offering in the presentation of the garden. Perhaps she is even moved to tears by the miracle of life that greets her. The second person, however, walks right by and never sees the garden. For him, *the garden wasn't there!* He will go through the rest of his life as if that garden never existed, so for him, you see, the world on that day did not have a garden. Although the same light and scent vibrations were available to both persons, the mind of the second person was not receptive to what creation was trying to reflect to him: the beauty of his own true nature. For the person who saw the garden and responded to it, a beautiful gift was received, a gift that profoundly opened her heart.

Perhaps you can remember having a difficult day, after which you decided to go for a walk. Perhaps you even stopped in front of a beautiful garden and had the experience of your stress simply dissolving.

In truth, an experience such as this can only happen because the garden was reminding you of your true nature. You realized that you needn't carry all the hard points of the day, nor must you deny them. There is a place for you to rest in between those two options, and that place has to do with how you see your world and how you *let yourself be seen* in the world.

Jesus, you will recall, told his followers not to hide their lights but to be like a lamp that is set on a pedestal that gives light to the whole room. Some consider that statement as mere poetic verbiage. Most will say, particularly on a difficult day, "I can't see my light. I don't even know if I have any light." Whether or not you actually see your own light is less important than *knowing* you *are* light. You came forth on a flow of goodness and wisdom, and there is simply no force or factor that can alter, negate or change that reality! You are a spark of your Source, which is *unimaginable* light, *unimaginable* sound, *unimaginable* presence! When you can smile and be at peace with yourself, even in the difficult moments, you substantiate your divine nature. That is all it takes to emanate light.

Engaging the Heart

Years ago, when I first instructed my students to think with their hearts and love with their heads, many became confused. However, over the years I have said it enough that most no longer react to the notion. Because it has been projected at you—and you accepted—that the head thinks and the heart loves, the notion that it could be the other way round produces a kind of cognitive dissonance. But what if the currently accepted projection turns out to be backward? What if you've been duped into believing that your mental energies are your thoughts (which most project to arise in the head) and your emotional energies are your feelings (which most project to arise in the heart)?

In truth, it is almost impossible to substantiate this projection, since your brain activity is heightened with the occurrence of both thoughts and feelings. Even so, such does not demonstrate where they come from. As you are perhaps beginning to notice, sooner or later you will have to challenge everything you believe if you are to transcend mind.

What if your heart created your schedule for the day? What if your heart determined your verbal responses to others? You see, the heart, when it is truly open, has no reason to distinguish between self and other. The heart, when it is open, loses the obsessive focus on itself and takes in the other.

Please note that I am not talking about your feelings. Those personal feelings arise from the solar plexus chakra, not the heart chakra. The job of the solar plexus is to let you know how the "I" is feeling. Do not confuse the "I" for the heart. When the heart is highly functional, it is wide open, and the difference between self and other simply dissolves into beautiful spaciousness. That wide-open heart could set your schedules, could decide the tone of your voice, could reach out, could even write your grocery list. By engaging the heart, you can give the head a vacation from all of the chores it sometimes hates. Much more than the head, the heart wants to preserve you for the benefit of everyone else.

You are here in physical form. You are needed here, and you are greatly loved! It is important that you recognize you have the capacity to become a Buddha. In fact, your hidden Buddha nature is trying to creep out from its secret place in your core. The only thing that stands in the way is the mind. When you come to see what really is—not just the appearances that arise—it is the mind that cuts through the illusion. In that case, the mind is no longer seen as the thinking apparatus. It is the heart that maintains connection to one's gut, so that instinctually one has access to the right movement, the right words. You do not have to think or feel about the situation ahead of time, preparing mental scripts. When the heart is open and available, you discover that you are in the midst of it rather than it being in the midst of you. From the heart, you emit a Buddha ray, or a Christ ray. When others receive it, often it changes how their mind projects or perceives you.

One of the kindest gifts you can offer to your family and friends is to begin seeing a Buddha in each of them. As you practice this way of seeing others, you will notice that the practice benefits them as well as you. The place to start is with those who irritate or frustrate you. In the East, when someone arises in your field of experiencing who triggers you emotionally, you say thank you because you know this one to be a manifestation of a Buddha. Why else would he or she go to all the trouble to show you where your emotional charges lie? Most people are quite self-occupied, living in the realm of their own making. But when a Buddha comes along, the charged areas you have managed to hide can get quite a workout. You find out where they are, and hopefully you are motivated to heal them. Thus, you say thank you.

Such is the gift of a Buddha in your life! Clearly, what you get out of the adventure is wholeness. What the other person gets out of it is the very powerful, positive energy of you projecting him or her as a Buddha. Sometimes it is just as simple as bowing to that person (inwardly, if not outwardly). Of course, it can be difficult for the ego to bow when you meet someone with whom you have a history of feeling frustration or irritation. What better opportunity to confront the ego and push through its force field into a clearer personal space? In other words, *act like a Buddha!*

Just because someone is showing you the appearance of a negative side does not mean that such is who he or she really is! A Buddha sees through the appearance and recognizes the Buddha potential in that one. The reactionary exchanges are but an illusion, and a Buddha sees right through them. The moment you acknowledge the illusion, you offer yourself an opportunity to see the person and the exchange differently. Often, as your energy shifts, a reciprocal shift may arise from the other as well.

Pay Attention to Your Projections

Every time you stumble into prickly situations, pose this question to yourself: "Does this seem real?" Or just utter the acknowledgment, "Things are not as they appear." Of course, the mind is ready to totally accept the appearance as the reality, so you will need to apply the practice of mindfulness to each situation in order to remember to ask the question. Perhaps you see a particular color and your mind will tell you, "This is green." You could, however, have an interesting argument trying to convince those who see the same color as blue.

As you know, the color turquoise is a color that some see as blue and some see as green, but both think they see it correctly. Your mind has, conveniently enough, convinced you that *your* projections are real; it is the other who sees the color incorrectly. However, in the final analysis, it turns out that projections of the mind are what stand between you and Buddhahood, for they obscure the vision of your Buddha eyes. Why should you believe that your projections, or those of another individual, are accurate? Indeed, what evidence do you have that your projections of *yourself* are accurate? The mind is projecting all the time, and it turns out that you not only project whatever the mind holds but you also receive the projections back again, perhaps interpreting them to be coming to you from "out there."

Others also absorb those projections, whether or not they understand the process, whether or not they agree with the thoughts being projected. If you project yourself as incapable, unwell, unlovable or just plain grumpy, others will absorb those projections and they will assume that those things are true of you. But under careful analysis, you have no evidence that these qualities are or even can be true of you. All you have is the projection of what you are feeling in a given moment, and as you know, that can quickly change. Therefore, it must not be true.

Indeed, it is extremely important to pay attention to what you project about yourself. If you feel upset or impatient, *you* might know that such is not your true self, but others might not know it. If you are generating those projections, others may simply accept the behavior as "you" because it is who you appear to be in the moment. You simply cannot expect others to see through appearances—that is your job. You must learn to challenge your perceptions but not necessarily reject them. It frequently turns out that the projections you think are right are the very ones that get you in trouble, for believing a projection locks you into the appearance.

As you begin your day tomorrow, go to your car and say, "This *appears* to be my car." As you get in, say, "It *appears* that this key will start the engine." Continue for a few days to focus on how things appear, acknowledging each appearance as it arises. When you feel accomplished with the basics, observe your relationships with the same intentional focus. Start acknowledging how these people appear to you. Just by saying to yourself, "This person *appears* to be very competent," or "This person *appears* to be angry," you acknowledge how your mind sees them—not how they are. Then acknowledge that what you see is a mental projection. This is not to say that what you see is wrong; it is rather to say that what you see is probably not all there is to see.

As you become accustomed to focusing on appearances, broaden the exercise. Acknowledge everything you perceive as an appearance.

Should you hear someone take a tone of voice that's disquieting to you, recognize that as an appearance. If you hear a tone of voice that is unsettling to you, recognize that you are the one who's putting a label on the tone. Such is how it appears to you, but *it might not be accurate*. Little by little you begin seeing through your mental projections. What you are seeing through is how your mind manipulates your "reality." It holds you separate from everything that appears. It holds that its moments of brilliance are different, indeed separate, from those of others, and it reinforces the notion of separation by designating itself an "I" distinct from all others.

Such is the ego mind's view of your "reality." However, there is absolutely no way you can go out into the universe and substantiate the mind's claim. Even if you understand the truth of that last statement, such does not make those mental projections less powerful as they arise.

When you consider a Buddha, one of the first qualities that comes to mind is often the unflappable tranquillity this one emanates. That all-abiding tranquillity arises from the recognition that every perception, every interaction, even every thought is but an appearance. When you comprehend fully the creative magnitude of this way of seeing the world, you realize there is no force "out there" that has the power to disturb your tranquillity. What could possibly jar your core enough to throw you off-center when you realize that the situations before you are but transitory appearances?

Therefore, the disruptions in your tranquillity must come from within the mind. You can release a tremendous load of stress from your life by acknowledging appearances and just remaining open to what they might mean. You need not treat your projections about the appearances as if they were real. Rather, you can stay open to the many potentialities that are arising in every moment.

You do not have to know what is really happening at a given moment to acknowledge how it appears. Perhaps it *appears* that someone is stalking you. It may *appear* that someone is trying to deceive you. It may even *appear* that someone is trying to steal your lover or your mate. By acknowledging what appears, you are able to bring attention to the situation rather than to the reactions that might arise if you actually believe your projections. In conventional reality, when the projections of several people seem to agree, you are more likely to believe the projections. Perhaps fifteen people say, "Yep, she's trying to get your husband." What they are confirming for you is not the accuracy of the projection. Rather, they are confirming that *they all have the karma to see the situation in the same way.* Just because numbers of people agree on the projection does not necessarily substantiate it.

Find Your Buddha Within

Although several people holding a similar perception in no way makes it accurate, neither does such make it inaccurate. What you must recognize is that the need to find a perception as accurate or inaccurate is a mental gyration, one that usually leaves the heart out of the process. To become a Buddha is to lose that compelling sense of being a separated self, which can be a bit precarious. If someone does something sweet or kind for you, normally you want to feel the good feelings that arise from the solar plexus. However, what a Buddha would be doing is looking at that other in compassion, seeing the beauty of his or her gift and delighting in the fact that that he or she is happy for giving it.

On the other hand, if someone flings what appears to be an insult at you, the ego mind wants to distance or put up protective walls. It wants to shut down the other individual in one way or another. What a Buddha experiences is looking at the person with great compassion, knowing that he could only hurl an insult because of his own pain. Were this one really alive and awake to his own pain, it would be impossible to insult another. To do so would only cause the individual more pain.

Remember, things are not as they appear. The one who hurls the insult is really the one who is in pain, even though she may be totally disconnected from her own pain level. If you (receiving the perceived insult) so chose, you can sink into a painful place also. But if you look through your Buddha eyes, you may discover that sometimes (perhaps always) pain is a choice. In practicing seeing through your Buddha eyes, you learn something about real freedom and you grow into your true nature, which is empty and spacious. As such, it has no personal agenda, since spaciousness allows grace to flow through without the personal reference point, or "I." Rather, there is only the outpouring of grace, which leads to wisdom and always produces kindness.

If you are going to see yourself as a Buddha, you must learn to pay attention to your thoughts and speech. You must learn to be a keen observer of your mind, both its thoughts and feelings, as well as the resulting words and actions that come forth. You will also learn to be tranquil within, even in difficult moments, for when a highly charged moment arises and you react from an emotionally charged place, you will quickly note that it is not the Buddha who speaks or thinks. Set your intentions to move in the world as one who is healed, and then go forward. Move in the world as would a Buddha, as one who demonstrates her spiritual lineage just by her carriage. Carry yourself with integrity. Carry yourself with a sense of vastness. Let your inner world be calm, and with your inner eye always focused on your teacher, rest in the magic of the grace and love your teacher affords you. Rest in that precious space, and let the mind be quiet.

Dedicate this year to seeing the Buddha within or the Christ within. Whether or not you fully accomplish this feat is less important than making the dedication to do so. Of course, it will not happen without your dedicated focus, and what better time to commit to your enlightenment than the present? Know that just as others before you have accomplished their enlightenment, so too can you. Take confidence in your path, and create your life accordingly. Cherish your life—you may never have another one quite like it. Recognize that this life is an opportunity to do something great, to create a healing for those old wounds and to give back to the Earth, or Mother Nature, who has afforded you passage so many times.

Learn how to love, *really* love! Love not from a perspective of a self, where the mind says, "I love you," but learn to become the very *field of love*. Allow divine love to flow through you, blessing the entirety of creation. In love, dedicate all your accomplishments to the benefit of all beings, that they too might stretch beyond the prison of the projecting mind.

2

Mind as Creator

You may remember the story of the young Greek man Narcissus, who looking into a stream, saw his image and was mesmerized by it. He was so captivated, in fact, that he couldn't bear to look away, let alone leave. He found the beauty of his own reflection so compelling and irresistible that, as the story goes, he fell in love with himself. As a punishment for being so self-absorbed, the gods turned him into a flower, so he could sit by the stream and view his reflection perpetually, rising in fresh elegance each and every spring.

In truth, this story really isn't a story of someone falling in love with himself. Rather, it is a story of someone falling in love with his image. Narcissus knew, of course, that he was staring at his own reflection, but he was so captivated by it and so compelled to keep looking at it, that days went by as he was lost in vanity. He neither ate nor slept. He adored his image in the sunlight and loved it in the moonlight. He simply could not release the image from his gaze.

Narcissism Is Very Seductive

Even though this is an old and familiar story, the issues it addresses are just as pertinent today as two thousand years ago. People today do still carry a strong fascination with their own images. However, in today's world, the fashion industry and the advertising industry have done everything possible to make people obsessed with those images. The idea is that if you just look good enough, nothing else matters.

The obsession with image has become a national force field, particularly designed to increase consumerism. The idea is to get people to spend money they do not really have for things they do not really need, with the end result that a few vendors get very rich.

For those who are unaware of the energy they are spending on supporting their images, there is really little to expect but physical and emotional exhaustion. Without a dose of consciousness being injected into the equation, the pattern will continue to play itself out day after day (perhaps lifetime after lifetime), with little awareness that one is being had by the social systems at play in a given time. Add consciousness to the mix, however, and things begin to change.

A deep part of the psyche begins to realize it has been had by the system that claims to support it. People awaken to the realization that they are giving their greatest effort and best energy to areas that either cannot or will not return the favor. With all the energy going to the world "out there," there may be little reserve left to nurture and inspire the deep inner regions of one's self and those one loves the most. This kind of awakening can be quite painful actually, leading to the depression and hopelessness for which the Western world is becoming all too well-known.

The more one opens the eyes of awareness, the more one sees how vapid is the rat race. If one then searches for deeper meanings, one must confront the call of the soul. As one begins to deepen into his or her life, seeking the reason he or she took birth in the first place, a spiritual path will arise to aid the individual in severing ties with the image or path of the false self. A search will begin for the true self, and the seeker will discover that if a spiritual path is to be genuinely approached, he or she can no longer allow the seduction and hypnotic spell of the false self. Rather, the narcissistic levels must be confronted if discovery of the real self is to emerge.

Remember, narcissism is very seductive. When one is really into the narcissistic projection, there is a kind of juice that starts flowing in the body. The brain is busy generating peptides that instruct the very cells to feel good about that image. Those little chemical agents can even get one to believe that the narcissistic image is the real thing. If one is rewarded over a period of time for the image one presents, it is likely that he or she will also become addicted to the chemical agents cascading through the body when feeling the image to be real. Breaking free from the control of these habituated "highs" can be a daunting task and requires a sophisticated understanding of both narcissism and spiritual narcissism.

In general, the narcissistic individual is totally wrapped up in himself or herself and appears self-serving at every turn. When you are with the narcissistic individual, you will be given repeated messages of one kind or another as to how wonderful he or she is. This personality is not difficult to recognize, and it may be demonstrated in varying degrees. The narcissist must have an image, and some have many, which can be brought out of the closet for the appropriate occasion.

The world "out there" blatantly and subtly encourages the formation of the image, since so many of the messages presented by the advertisers have the net effect of instilling and heightening a self-consciousness that promotes consumerism. The lure is that if one looks "right," possesses the "right" toys, gives the "right" answers, travels to all the "cool" spots and rubs elbows with the "cool" people, he or she will experience the good life. The message left out, of course, is that the advertisers will never let you feel like you have enough material things (i.e., stuff) or cool experiences. The image that buys into this kind of manipulation can never be satiated.

Narcissism and Spirituality

Although one might expect such to be a part of the world, it becomes a bit more interesting when it creeps into spirituality. As one makes the journey inward, the task is to discover who is hiding behind the images the ego is fond of presenting. Do not think that a spiritual path exempts one from the grasp of the ego! Even on the spiritual path, sometimes the "right" image gets confused with the true self one seeks to know. The nature of the ego is such that its powerful hold on the image can confuse the becoming self.

Tradition to tradition, spirituality has always afforded seekers the opportunity to cut through the array of false selves each may have amassed through the journey of countless lives. Although practices vary tradition to tradition, the transformative goal is essentially the same: to experience the divine within oneself. The nature of the journey is such that the opportunities to cut through the false self are often also opportunities to fall into the false self. Such being the case, the spiritual journey may seem to be replete with wrong turns, confusing maps, even dead-end routes. It is the systematic working through of the lessons learned and dedication to ruthless self-investigation, however, that open the door to the cessation of suffering.

Spiritual narcissism can manifest in many ways. It can look like arrogance, for example, as when someone announces, "This is my last life!" If it really were the person's last life, it is doubtful that the idea to announce it would ever arise into consciousness. It is very ego-centered to always be worried about whether this may be the last life. Although the ego might get plenty of mileage out of the preoccupation, no other part of consciousness is expanded by it. In fact, quite the opposite is going on, and the fixation itself is a type of ego superiority.

The antidote for spiritual narcissism is the bodhisattva path, wherein one continually practices taking oneself off the ego's screen, replacing the focus on others. Yet even in this practice, one must be careful. The potential exists to do even this level of spiritual practice from an egoic or self-centered motivation. One may take pride in how well he or she is doing the practice. One may use the practice to elevate a pseudohumility that is actually rooted in arrogance. Additionally, one might find special meaning in this practice if one has a codependent nature. Both such motivations could, from outward appearances, appear altruistic. Thus, one must diligently apply intelligence ruthlessly in the investigation of what the ego is pursuing at all times.

Although pride might be rather tricky to see through, if that is your issue, codependence may be even trickier. Codependence is less straightforward because it is supported by one form of denial or another. The problem with denial, however, is that it seldom stands alone. Denial always covers a predilection for addiction, whether out-and-out substance abuse, sexual addictions, buying addictions, addictions to habituated thoughts and feelings, addictions to reactionary behaviors, even addictions to chemicals one's own brain produces with varying emotional states. The bodhisattva path, of course, requires constant vigilance in rooting out even the subtlest of denial tendencies.

Glamour is another form of spiritual narcissism. Some get stuck in the glamour of past lives, whereas others find glamour in having a particular teacher. There are some who experience the glamour of being part of a spiritual community or of their spiritual lineage, thinking theirs to be a little better than that of others. These notions can actually take one into deeper levels of narcissism, rather than deeper levels of self-discovery. An inner struggle may arise when you as a seeker discover that the "who" you experience yourself to be and the "who" you think you are supposed to be lack consistency. The ego prefers to glamorize the latter and ignore the former, which can get in the way of making the kind of progress the seeker desires.

You may have experienced some incredibly narcissistic beliefs spread by those who think they truly understand physical healing. Certain of these beliefs have become regarded as spiritual tenets, but in the end they are traps, because no one can ultimately succeed with them. You may hear something like, "Why do you have that disease? You're not thinking the right kind of thoughts. What's wrong with your life that you have this disease?" Or perhaps you've heard this one: "Well, if you have heart disease, it's because you don't know how to love." Although this stance may sometimes have a grain of truth, more often it obscures or leaves out altogether the value of the lessons, both for the one who manifests the disease and also for those connected to that one.

You can also see the infusion of the American image in "pop spirituality." The American image touts being successful, looking good and having everything go well enough so the ego is never confronted. When such is superimposed on spirituality, it can actually prove dangerous. It can be incredibly disheartening and failure-producing to hold up an image of success as the world knows it for some measure of spiritual accomplishment. The image I'm referring to says: "If you're not rich, if you're not beautiful, if you don't have the world by the tail, you're not spiritual."

Another form of spiritual narcissism may be found in spiritual laziness—or as the Christians term it, sloth. If the image of the spiritual self is in the driver's seat and one is feeling as though he or she is looking pretty spiritual to self and others, it may appear to the ego as if it can simply slide by. It might justify its stance by convincing itself that the rigorous investigation needed to discover the authentic self is probably just another obsession, and since engaging an obsession is just another form of addiction, why risk it? "I can coast by and not look bad. No one is going to know anyway." What can happen, however, is a rather interesting split in the mind. The split is between what one aspires to be and what one fears he or she is (or may be). The former needs no image, but the latter sorely needs an image, since it is clear that this part of the ego does not believe in itself. It is calling itself a fraud all the time.

This split in awareness is directly related to the presence of the narcissistic fixation on the image. It raises a kind of self-consciousness that is all absorbing. However, such is not the same as self-reflection, and instead of facilitating the seeker, it can actually become a significant impediment to the journey. The self-conscious individual needs the image (or so the ego argues), but that is because the ego has a bad habit of continually trying to con the self. The con—"I will hold to the image; no one will know"—lies in the fact that this ego is ardently attempting *not* to see the self, *not* to look deeply to find and dissolve the obscurations that block the experience of authenticity. Yet at the same time, it professes to be on the path of spiritual discovery.

The Image Mask Is But an Imitation of the True Self

Certainly, we could list other examples of spiritual narcissism, and we could delve more deeply into the pitfalls of the mask or image. The real question, however, is why might it ever occur to humanity to rely on an image in the first place? To what is this image mask likened? For what is it a substitute? Perhaps the perceived need for the mask or the image is based in some egoic belief that one is disconnected from whatever is real. The presence of the image mask serves only to substantiate that one is somehow separated from the divine. In the pain of this perceived separation, the ego—which is the part that experiences separation—creates an image mask to divert its attention from the pain it feels. Thus, the image mask is but an imitation of the real or higher self.

What must be remembered is the fact that the physical state is not your natural state; it is your disguise. Taking physical form is much like going to a costume party. Everyone puts on a disguise—a personality and a body—and attends the party looking for all their friends. You and everyone else see who you can recognize. When the party is over, you take off your costume, rest awhile, and you go again. Perhaps in the next life you put on a different costume, and once again you look for your friends. Sometimes you look for your enemies, and sometimes they find you. Although the physical presentation may be as close as you can come in the realization process right now, still, it is not your authentic self.

Ultimately, you learn that you are not just a physical-psychological being, because after the physical-psychological parts disappear, there is something still aware—even after a thousand lifetimes come and go. Your disguises are many. You use different nationalities, different genders, different social and economic levels. In review, you look at all the disguises and you say, "They're all different—very, very different." But underneath them all there is something that is the same: your authentic self. That authentic self is what everybody is trying to discover, but if you are estranged from that self, the image masks seem necessary.

Entering a lifetime makes you and everyone else a target for the projections of those around you. You enter a life, and parents start telling you who you are. Some even tell you what you are supposed to become. They tell you what's right and what's wrong. They tell you what's good about you; they tell you what's bad about you. Frequently they say more about the bad than they say about the good, and you become the recipient of their projections. However, these projections have nothing to do with your essence.

As a little child, you begin to believe the projections are true, having no way to invalidate them. I remember what one father said about his son a few years ago. He had a young boy who was very, very bright, scoring 180 or 190 on IQ tests. The child was also quite high-strung. In the presence of the boy, the father would say, "He'll be president some day if they don't hang him first."

Considering those options, it is no wonder the child grew but never actualized the full potential of his high intellect. If you stop and think how many people come and go, the odds of a given person becoming president are pretty slim, and you can figure that out at about ten or twelve years of age. Since the only other option projected on him was death by hanging, he was never able to accomplish his enlightenment potential. He was brilliant, but he lived his life in an emotional hole because he didn't want to be hanged. The projection, of course, started as a joke. The dad did get a lot of laughs from people, but when you think of the projection, it is staggering.

Another father used to introduce his son in this manner: "This is Ricky; he's slow in math." That projection followed Ricky all the way through his formal education—which, you might guess, was short. What can often be observed with children is the fact that others tend to put *their* masks on children. Most children never have the freedom to just discover who they are because they are so busy fighting off the projections of what a parent or first-grade teacher told them.

When the parent's (or other adult's) way of seeing gets projected onto the child's experience, it alters the way his or her expectations manifest. As the child tries to learn how to be in the world, it takes some skillful handling from the adults to teach discrimination between appropriate and inappropriate behavior. That is, after all, what the parent's job is. But in the meantime, most are also projecting all over the child, altering his or her creative field.

Coming into one's own aliveness requires throwing off the projections that one has collected—often unknowingly—from others in his or her surroundings. How many projections might one collect in two or three thousand lives? No wonder the image mask becomes so important a tool to the ego!

If I ask you how you are, you can answer easily. If I ask you *who* you are, it becomes much more interesting. Most, in fact, do not really know. Not knowing may seem a bit strange, but it is not a bad thing at all. Not knowing can keep you curious, if you don't go to sleep. To show up in your life and be curious about who you are, to really look at what's behind this image or this composite, can be a powerful transformative exercise.

That natural curiosity to want to know essence is in everyone, and the way it manifests is in a drive to be whole. The great movement (perhaps a surprise) is when the mind wakes up and one has an enlightenment experience, breaking through those powerful projections. The entire life experience is seen for what it *really* is—a projection. None of it is real. It feels real, it seems real, it even functions as a reality. However, it is all a huge mental projection.

To better grasp this idea, imagine for a moment that you are standing inside a white column, the inside of which is lined with the material used on a projection screen. Think of your mind as a movie projector that is capable of producing a 360-degree image. On the screen before, around and behind you appear the projections of your mind—both your history and the future context your mind holds. The beliefs and perceptions of your past experiences provide the symbols and emotional content, or what you believe to be going on in your life right now.

Observe that in all the battles you fight, the repeating occurrences and patterns in your life are but projections from your mind. As long as you continue to fight your projections or reenact the old patterns, the story line simply cannot change. You will see the old and the familiar arising again and again, seemingly coming to you from your experiences "out there." Careful observation, however, reveals that the "out there" you have accepted is coming from the "in here" from which you project. The goal is to cut through that screen and see what your experience of creation might be without your projections.

When you cut through, the brilliance is so profound that you no longer need an image. In fact, that light of your being is so bright, it dissolves anything that obscures your authentic radiance. You learn to identify more and more with the observer—which, you discover, is your link to the divine. Inside you, somewhere hidden from the mind, is the point of light where essence is anchored. Essence is watching. The mind, however, is so defined by *doing* that it forgets about the part that is *watching*. Although doing is important on the physical plane, don't confuse the doing for the real self.

Artificial Connections with Others

Thus, the lesson is great. You may be worried about your image, but that is only what is going on in your mind. Others are already carrying an image of you, and they are busy relating to it more than they are relating to what you think you are projecting (i.e., your image mask). If you are honest with yourself, you will realize that you do the same to others. You project the thought, "Oh, he is giving me this gift because he really loves me." Or, "She's giving me this gift because she feels guilty about something." Or, "He's giving me this gift because he is reciprocating for something I gave him." All these thoughts are projections! The projections get in the way of receiving the gift and showing up for the exchange.

Suppose you enroll in a class and you haven't been in a class for a number of years. On the first day, the teacher asks a question and you answer it. Perhaps the teacher pauses and is a little meditative about your answer. Watch the mental projections arise! "Oh, he thinks that's a good answer." Or, "Oh, I bet I gave the wrong answer and he thinks I'm stupid." The projections are going on all of the time, and they get in the way of authentic connections. You do get information energetically, but the real test is to stay with the energy and not let the mind get into ascribing meaning to the energy. Such will only lead you into the realm of projection.

Living in a culture where a spiritual ideal is held up as a fashionable image is very tricky. Some people will think, "I'm more spiritual if I can model the good life." Be careful of the temptation to believe that adage. As you learn to show up more and more for your own life as you move toward the ruthless self-examination of the bodhisattva, you begin to see clearly the hidden power of projections. Usually you see the power of others' projections before you see how powerful your own are. At first glance, projections aren't so obvious. Nearly everyone has come to accept them as valid. What you ultimately discover when you whittle away all your own projections is that all those people in your life are not relating to you at all. They're relating to their *projections* of you. You recognize that you have been doing the same thing with/to them. Once you see through this artificial way of connecting, you simply cannot continue relating as projection to projection.

When someone steps onto your screen whom you've known for fifteen years who suddenly acts in an outrageous way, have you ever noticed that you can't project on him or her? You have to show up and say, "What's going on?" You find you are shocked out of your projective trance and you see with fresh eyes. The important thing is that you break the trance that results from projections bouncing off other projections. It is precisely with regard to such trance states that the Buddha yelled, "Wake up!"

Waking Up from Your Mind Trance

The mind asleep is like other forms of trance. For some, the trance may be light, whereas for others it can be quite heavy. In such a case, although not impossible, the likelihood of waking up is more remote. When you recognize that it is those mental projections that create the trance—that hypnotic, checked-out sleepiness in which so many live their lives—then the desire to get an authentic experience of oneself becomes precious and highly motivating.

Although it may not be completely clear as yet, you will eventually awaken to the tactics the mind uses to create and perpetuate trance states through continual projecting activity. In truth, until a trance becomes obvious, it remains completely hidden from the individual in the trance. If you have ever observed a stage hypnotist's presentation, you can draw an analogy that is useful in our work here. In the stage hypnotist's production, normally audience members remain "awake," or not under the influence of the trances the hypnotist works on his subjects. While his presentations are generally given for their entertainment value, they also teach a great deal about what is generally deemed to be the normal waking state of consciousness.

A Buddha would hold that this "normal" state is no less influenced by trance states than are those used on subjects for the stage hypnotist's production. For example, the hypnotist might instruct a person in a trance to confuse marbles and jacks. Then, upon directing the person to return to her normal waking state, he then asks her to name objects lying on a table nearby. The viewer observes the power of the trance, since even after "waking up" the person confuses marbles and jacks.

The reason such a trick seems funny is because most people cannot understand how someone who appears to be present and awake, and who never confused marbles and jacks previously, operates under that trance of confusion. Yet if you carefully observe yourself and others, you will see that people go into trances of confusion all the time—even when there is no hypnotist to induce a trance. In truth, it is the force of one's own karmic proclivities that induces the trances that arise in the ongoing process of cyclic existence. Indeed, this is precisely what the Buddha saw, and it is why his perennial calls to "Wake up!" are so powerful today, some two thousand plus years after his physical presence on Earth.

Like the stage hypnotist to his subjects, you are continually giving yourself suggestion from the *bakchaks* (karmic imprints) you carry from your past. Like the subjects in the hypnotist's show, your mind is highly suggestible—that is, it readily responds to the suggestions it receives. The only difference is that in one's personal life, there is no external hypnotist to blame for one's own trances, nor are there any external subjects of the trance to observe from a humorous perspective. Although the pattern is identical, all of the activity and hypnotic exchange is going on within the self. When you are engaged in giving yourself hypnotic suggestions (via karmic imprint), you will discover that this function of mind often arises in a very subtle manner—perhaps as a matter of habit.

Can you remember a time when you really wanted to impress someone you were meeting for the first time? If you were nervous or uncertain enough, you may have had the experience of what seemed like a forty-point IQ drop when in the person's presence! You may have been unable to recall what you wanted to say, or you might have begun to stutter, or perhaps some other trance took over that you *knew* was not normal for you. Simply stated, you gave yourself some suggestion, and taking the suggestion as truth, you moved right into a trance. If you have ever had the experience of looking right at something on the table before you and not seeing it—your wallet, say, or your keys—you were in the trance state that professional hypnotists call negative hallucination, or being unable to see something that is actually right there in front of you. For some, this is a common trance, and once habituated, it will replicate itself even if the one in the trance has no memory or recognition of giving oneself a suggestion.

The opposite of negative hallucination is, of course, positive hallucination, a trance state wherein one sees something physically exist when it does not. An example of this might be the projection of a paranoid individual—one who believes a federal agent is covertly following him. In this case, the hypnotic trance can be so strong that the person may be able to give a very detailed description of the projected federal agent, even though no such person is involved whatsoever.

Another trance state that is popular with stage hypnotists is the trance state of amnesia. On stage, the person may have been given the suggestion to forget her own name. Then after "waking," when the person is asked her name, she is unable to recall it. Again, what appears funny on stage may not be so funny in the course of one's personal experience. Thus, if one obsesses about how bad his memory is becoming, he creates a trance state in which his memory literally *has* to decline further. In like manner, projections fraught with worry, anxiety, fear, anger, guilt and so on constitute powerful suggestions that generate very strong trance states.

For many in the West, a widely experienced trance is that of continually staying busy. Although it is true that life in the current age on planet Earth seems filled with a vast array of compelling tasks and obligations that demand attention or so it seems, the obsession of busyness has become nearly universally accepted as the natural state. But all too often, the pressure that supports the obsession comes from within the individual experiencing the trance rather than from the apparent outside circumstances the overly busy individual tends to blame. Even though busyness has become a compelling way of life for many, it still should not be a reason for avoiding the work of cutting through the mind's habits. If you cannot penetrate the projections you hold of yourself, then those projections—as well as the ones you place on others—will continue to create the façade that ends up being your image mask. If you cannot penetrate your own mask, you cannot expect anybody else to see your true self. Likewise, you cannot expect that you will show up in a genuine enough way to really see who anybody else is either.

Getting to Genuine Authenticity

The assignment, of course, is getting to genuine authenticity. There are many, many meditation techniques that make invaluable contributions, but the real path is ruthless—and I do mean *ruthless*—self-examination. Such is how you penetrate your wounded psyche beyond even the most subtle of projections. You find yourself simply residing in a state of "don't know." Although many fear this condition, it can be quite exhilarating, since all those projections you've been carrying are amazingly heavy. A state of buoyancy, both physically and emotionally, arises when you let the projections go.

The more you let go, the more you tap your essential nature, which allows you to drop the costume you wear. The problem is not with your essential nature but your lifetimes and lifetimes of the narcissistic manipulation that egos create to feel secure, in control and accepted. Getting to know essence, however, will bring you home to your authentic divine nature and relieve you of those tiring, boring image masks. Essence reveals its magnificence to you in those quiet, inspiring moments when you are One with all creation, knowing the infinite ocean of love that literally *wants* to pour through you.

In my lives as a physical being, the most precious thing I got from my spiritual teachers was the gift of learning how to love. In every life, I thought I knew love or at least knew something about it. But in every case, I learned I knew nothing in comparison to the love my teacher demonstrated. I'm not being self-deprecating here; such is simply the truth. In the light of one teacher, I learned how to love at the length of, say, twelve inches, a foot. Then perhaps in a succeeding life, I would find myself in the company of a teacher who had a ten-foot love, and I would manage to stretch my love capacity to, say, two and a half feet. In a following life, I would find a teacher whose love would expand to twenty feet, and I would learn I could manage love at five feet. This example is very simplistic—for love, of course, is not linear, nor can it be measured in linear terms. However, there is a sense of continual moving as one expands into love, for in touching love deeply or in being touched deeply by great love, one's heart is profoundly expanded and healed.

Love Is Your Essential Nature

Each of you is a teacher to someone, perhaps many. You must clear away your own tendency to project on those who learn from you before expecting them to release their projections. Become enlightened as a way of loving and supporting them. Discover your luminosity so that they may discover theirs. Love them exquisitely, relentlessly and profoundly, so they too can deepen their capacity for love.

The spiritual training by which I made my greatest points of personal transcendence was the Buddhist tradition (although I was also Hindu and Taoist in a number of lives). Of particular significance were my lifetimes in Tibet, where we were taught that everyone we met was probably our parent in a previous life and thus we were taught to treat all with respect and serve each one as you would an aging parent. Now, whether or not one takes that teaching literally, it is helpful to your spiritual progress to treat *every* sentient being (even the animals) as if each cared for you in the past when you were young and vulnerable. In so doing, you get to see yourself giving them kindness for the kindness they previously gave to you.

We were also taught to care for the spiritual teacher as if we were the parent and the teacher was a little child. This way of thinking and behaving brings out a sense of protectiveness for the teacher and demonstrates the preciousness one feels for the teachings. In the West, sometimes it appears to me as if the students believe— even expect—that the teacher should care for them. The student often projects on the teacher an expectation of, "It's your job to look out for me, take care of me and, above all, see that I am loved unequivocally by you." As a spiritual practice, you might benefit from trying to see it the other way around.

Both of these practices are excellent for cutting through projections, and they add multiple dimensions to your capacity to love as well. Learn not to worry over whether you are or have been loved enough. Rather, concern yourself with whether you love enough. The most basic of human needs is not to *be* loved but to *love unboundedly*. Love has the power to dissolve all the image masks an ego can engage. Love is your essential nature. And when you love enough, you know God.

3

How Karma Works

A solid understanding of karma is essential for freeing oneself from suffering. It is also most useful in understanding basic relational dynamics, for karma is largely responsible for creating them. Sometimes called the law of cause and effect, the playing out of karma really amounts to the superimposition of the past on the present moment. Your thoughts and actions, both positive and negative, result from past karma but influence your future thoughts and actions as well. Karma is said to ripen when the effect of some prior cause erupts in the present. In that instant, free will is lost to the forcefulness of the emerging response or reaction.

This ripening comes from an energetic flow that was set in force perhaps lifetimes ago. Here I would like to take you to the deepest explanation or definition of karma. When we slip beneath the glib answers to the karma question, we must note that karma is *any movement of the mind*. To take a deeper and hopefully more functional definition, however, we must understand how karma and the mind are completely dependent on each other.

Initial Thought and Developing Thought

If we investigate just how the mind moves, we discover that there are two mind functions that need attention. The first is what we will call *initial thought*, and the other is *developing thought*. Initial thought is simply the function of wrapping your awareness around the situations and circumstances that arise in the landscape of your life. For example, imagine for a moment that you are about to cross a street. As you are stepping from the curb into the street, you notice a car is coming toward the crossing, going faster than it should. A startle response arises, and you realize that if you continue into the crosswalk, the oncoming speeding car will hit you.

Usually, the impressions you make with initial thought are accurate. As a result of collecting the data of the moment and organizing it, you are able to wait until the car clears the crosswalk before stepping into the street. Initial thought is useful for negotiating the world. It helps you understand the energetic forces coalescing in the moment, allowing you to make appropriate decisions.

Developing thought, however, is another matter. Developing thought is what you do at a personal level with the information taken in and assimilated through initial thought, or the way the mind moves with the information. Let us return again to the example given above to demonstrate moving mind, or developing thought. As you realize you are in the way of potential harm (the oncoming car), you become more alert and decide to step back on the curb until the car passes. As it does so, you may find yourself scrutinizing the driver of the vehicle. You look at the expression on the driver's face. Perhaps you become aware of the driver's age, gender and race. Taking in the information and making sense of it is using initial thought. However, as the mind moves, perhaps you get angry and think, "That idiot nearly killed me!" Suddenly, blame arises and you may feel victimized, even though nothing happened to you and you are as healthy as you were the moment before you saw the car.

With the movement of your mind, perhaps you focus on getting the license number so you can phone the police. Perhaps you did not like the expression on the driver's face and your mind decided he was angry, hostile or perhaps had a chip on the shoulder. Perhaps you noticed that the car was a red sporty model, and the mind gave you the thought, "You're never safe in the vicinity of a red sports car with a young male driver!" All this activity, although quite stimulating, even interesting, is developing thought. The mind moves in a direction consistent with past experiences and creates a story that is self-serving in one way or another. These mental movements happen so quickly that you may not realize the mind has moved into developing thought. If perchance you know someone who was hit by a speeding car, the mind might move in that direction, comparing the present moment with what happened to the other person or fantasizing that what happened to your acquaintance could happen to you.

As you look deeply into your own karmic projections, you will undoubtedly discover that your mind has consistent patterns of movement. For example, you may have had a number of lifetimes where you had difficulty with authority figures of one kind or another. Of course, it is impossible for you to remember the experiences of your past lives, but if you have issues with authority today, it is likely you are dragging some old unresolved energy into the now. Consequently, whenever you have a brush with an authority figure, you suffer. You may suffer anything from mild irritation, to smoldering resentment, to a volcanic-like eruption at the fact that someone is telling you what to do. Your mind will tend to project in a way that is consistent with the interpretations you have placed on similar experiences in the past.

Don't Confuse the Karma with the Person

In the process of investigating situations in your life, whatever the interpretation may be that you place on any event, what you are actually viewing (or reviewing) is your karma. Perhaps you can recall a moment when you told a lie and within fifteen minutes you were internally castigating yourself, wondering why your mind moved in the direction of lying to the other person. What you are witnessing is the ripening of a piece of karma. What arose in that moment, from the standpoint of probability, was a stronger potential to tell a lie than to tell the truth. You were not forced to tell the lie, for you could have sidestepped the rising karmic influence and told the truth.

In such a situation, developing thought can move quickly into action, giving you all the reasons you couldn't tell the truth. The mind says, "It would hurt the person's feelings if I told the truth, and I surely don't want to do that!" Or, "If I told the truth, it would complicate the situation unnecessarily. I would have so much explaining to do that it's just easier to tell the lie." Another form of developing thought might be to continue to castigate yourself for having told the lie (rather than simply apologize), obsessing on what this behavior really means with regard to you. Developing mind could chew on that one for days!

Perhaps you can recall an occasion when a loved one needed to confess something to you that was causing her to suffer. Perhaps the confession shocked you. Perhaps you were told the person stole something, or cheated on a lover, or embezzled money at work. In your shock, you may have thought she was telling you something about herself. Developing mind might have entered the picture, and perhaps you felt judgmental of the other. It is *very* important that you hold yourself to a strong standard of integrity. *Don't confuse the karma for the person!*

In other words, the confessor was only telling you *her* karma. The very fact that you became shocked when you heard the confession demonstrates that she was not telling you something about herself. If she confesses embezzlement, it is very easy for developing mind to conclude that she is a thief. However, were that true, then likely the need to confess would not arise, since thieves seldom have episodic bouts of remorse and truth telling.

Confusing the karma for the person is rather like confusing the driver for the vehicle. Developing mind *loves* this one! Imagine you have just driven your car into the garage of a shopping center. As you are just about to open the door to exit your car, a huge Humvee roars into the spot next to you, perhaps even soundly startling you. Developing mind reminds you that you know what kind of person that is. "One of those militant types," you hear inwardly. Or, "One of those environmentally irresponsible types driving in here in her personal tank, for god's sake!" The mind takes off, and you suffer. If you allow it, the event could ruin the rest of your day.

Confusing the karma with the person is, of course, to misunderstand karma. It is a mistake—sometimes a grave mistake—to confuse a person (self or other) with the movement of the mind. In a very real sense, until one awakens, one cannot help where the mind goes. One must first awaken to the fact that one *does* have some input into the thoughts and images the mind holds. Conventionally speaking, most do not think they can alter how they think or feel in a given situation. The feelings arise, the thoughts occur, before one is aware of thinking or feeling. Therefore, most believe that thoughts and feelings must be valid, and exist outside the realm of one's control.

Westerners Are in a Most Auspicious
Life for Working through Karma

As you learn to work with karmic projections of the mind, you may become overwhelmed from time to time with just how vast the karmic ocean is. In these moments, what you are actually feeling is the pressure of all of the lifetimes that have left some kind of a karmic imprint on your awareness. At your spiritual core, you feel a desire for freedom from the mental tyranny that emerges from and with karmic imprints. Yet those imprints are etched so deeply into the psyche that they are literally out of reach for the conscious mind. This recognition may lead to a "have to/can't" struggle with regard to releasing the imprints.

Most people have at least one painful personal area that they would like to change. Often a significant part of the pain comes from the fact that they feel helpless to effect change in that area. It is flawed thinking to hope that the problem will change if the karma remains. Left intact, those karmic imprints will override your best efforts, your best intentions, every time. The more a particular projection has been reinforced in your past lives, the deeper the imprinting. The deeper the imprinting, the greater the insight required to break free.

A commonly held belief is that the cutting-through process should be easier than it actually is. It probably seems that if you could just see clearly the healed state and if you desire that state enough, the state should simply materialize on the basis of: (1) your intention to have it, and (2) the flash of clarity you had when you grasped the healed state. When you recognize that you are creating with your projections, you may diligently apply massive doses of affirmations to the problem area, hoping to change an attitude or habit of mind. In fact, the problem may move to a subtler level so that you have to look a little more diligently to find it. Or the work you have done might cause the problem to go underground. If so, it will eventually arise again because the karma hasn't yet been cleared.

It is important to recognize that if you are living this life in the Western world, you are in a most auspicious life for working through your karma. Westerners have many gifts that others miss who experience living in other parts of the world. For example, in the West you have become accustomed to having leisure time. In many other parts of the world, however, people find that all their energies are required to scratch out an existence and thus have little or no time nor energy left to pursue a spiritual path. Likewise, here in the West you have access to many, many teachings in the form of books. Further, there are many spiritual teachers moving to the West because of persecution in their own native regions. Having such access to both spiritual teachers and profound teachings is something you must never take for granted. Rather, commit to responsibly utilizing the gifts of your present life, and dedicate the fruits of all your spiritual accomplishments for the benefit of all who may not have access to the abundance of spiritual gifts available to you.

One of the theories about karma that might be useful for you to consider would be analogous to a bank account. In your karma account, you save or store your good karma. You are free to spend that karma anytime you have enough to "buy" a good life. In other words, if you have a life that is relatively easy when compared to world standards, you have it as a result of accumulating good karma from your past experiencing. Although this analogy is simplistic, it can be helpful nonetheless.

Consider for a moment areas of the world where the population is the highest. Clearly, these are the places where more people are born, and as you know, the field of experiencing in areas of dense population with limited food and resources can be quite harsh. As you look at what is the normal experience for most of the people on Earth, how much good karma do you think you have spent to procure this life?

If you are a Westerner, you have the karma to avail yourself of innovative medical procedures. In fact, you will not even be exposed to physical conditions that literally ravage much of the world's population. For the diseases and conditions you do contract, you have access to care and comfort, powerful drugs and innovative techniques that would seem incredible to most people on the planet. With compassion, think of how many suffering people will never in an entire life know the comforts you may take for granted.

When you consider how fortunate you are just in terms of that to which you have access, you will recognize that you are among the most fortunate of the world. By appreciating what you have—even if you paid for it all from your karma account—you generate a positive force in your own karmic continuum. Not only should you pause daily to think about your fortunate birth and appreciate it, you should also appreciate the fact that you are using up good karma. Therefore, it is important that you use the gifts you have purchased with your positive karma to refill your account. When you have access to a teacher and solid spiritual teachings, and when you also have the time to study the teachings and live them, then require yourself at the very least to be awake enough to realize how precious this particular life is.

Having made mention of all the above considerations, never be arrogant about your life circumstances, no matter how persuasive the ego. Rather, recognize that if you have a life of relative ease, you took it so that you could serve others who might have a more difficult situation to bear in the ripening of their karma. Indeed, *all* circumstances should point your focus in the direction of compassion and generosity. Do not mistake a "good life" as meaning others owe you something. In truth, the easier the conditions of a life, the greater energy, focus and commitment you can apply to easing the suffering of all other sentient beings.

Karma Also Manifests through the Body

From a spiritual perspective, it is useful to consider with some regular frequency that you are dying. Pay attention to the fact that things will not go on forever as they now are. In truth, you began dying the moment you took birth. Be aware that what you have in this life is sure to change. Your body is changing right now; in fact, it changes with every breath you take. Your relationships must change, for sooner or later death will catch some of those you love. Your mind will continue to undergo changes until you eventually exit your body.

When you take physical form, you do so in order to see karma manifest that it might be cleared. And as some healer types are fond of saying, "Those issues are in the tissues." Literally, your cells are energetically encoded by your karma just as is your mind. You might say this is a fail-safe system, for if you miss the karmic imprints in the mind, karma can still manifest through the body, giving you another opportunity to approach it. Periodically, it is important to drop the cells with their karmic encoding, and death provides a convenient exit strategy. Part of the change you reference as aging is due to the effects of working through the encoding on the physical cells. Generally speaking, the cells also pay a price for liberation.

Karma sees to it that most people do experience aging. Although there is value to the aging process, do not think such is the only way life in a body can be experienced, for there have been those who maintained a single body for over a thousand years. Since the latter condition is not likely for most people, just know that if you experience yourself as aging, then it is your karma to do so. Rather than fighting your karma, try to observe the process with curiosity and be as gentle as you can be with the body as it goes through its changes.

In the West, it is a commonly held projection that athleticism is heightened in the twenties or thirties but inevitably starts to decline thereafter. Those who believe such are demonstrating that they have the karma to see/understand life in such terms. When entire social structures see in these terms, the collective projections become accepted as "truth," notwithstanding that other cultures have demonstrated—and have therefore held as "truth"—that the greatest level of athletic prowess comes not in the twenties but in the fifties. Those steeped in the collective projection of the former (that athleticism is highest in the twenties) will be shocked to discover what was "true" for older cultures living high in the Andes Mountains only a few generations ago.

Mastering Karma Requires Challenging Your Own Mind

When we speak in terms of your karma, we are referring to how your mind moves with the experiences in your life. When you pay attention to the movement you witness in the minds of others, little by little you will begin to understand how their karmic patterns arise. As in your own case, often others cannot see their own patterns arise. This is because the karma they carry functions as a kind of template in the mind, restricting access to only a limited range of possibilities. That template is etched in the awareness by the karmic imprints, which were formed by past experiences and interpretations. Thus, the mind is conditioned to move in such a way as to replicate those patterned ways of seeing lifetime after lifetime. It is not until one awakens to this fact that one has the opportunity to alter the mind's movement. Until one awakens to the genuine creative power of the mind, there can be little experience of personal empowerment and the habituated ways of seeing replicate in one's experiences over and over.

This repetitive reinforcing of patterned ways of seeing allows us to consider such emotional states as hatred. Simply stated, the more reinforcement a notion of separation has had, the stronger the hatred. If one has the karma to detest a particular race, gender or social strata, the relative level of energy the charge of hatred bears gives evidence to the power of imprint reinforcement. What might have begun a thousand lifetimes ago as some emotional wounding, if reinforced enough, can arise with profound implications in the present life. Therefore, should you encounter those who seem filled with hatred, remember that they are simply showing you their karma.

Clearly, mastering karma requires challenging your own mind. You will have to ask yourself again and again, "Why do I see it this way?" Or, "Why do I see blue as a beautiful color and brown as an ugly color?" There is, of course, no innate beauty or ugliness in the color, and a rising judgment is only the movement of your mind, which has much more to do with what you associate with that color than with something coming from the color itself. If you investigate the interpretations associated with all your preferences, you will likely discover something profound about your karma.

If you suddenly began questioning every thought at the moment of its arising, the world would appear quite different to you. Just the fact of being awake enough to investigate your perceptions and projections would cause you to see whole strata of experiencing you have previously missed. There will very likely come a time in your spiritual development when you will question your every thought. Your mind will project a notion, and you will immediately recognize the notion as illusion.

You will laugh right out loud at your mind, seeing both the fallacy of the projection and the wonder of how the mind projects/creates. "How does my mind project this thought? I've just seen it *again!* I thought that person rejected me, but in actuality it was I who projected my fear of rejection on him and received it back, believing it was coming from him!" You will see rejection arise, even though you know another cannot reject you. You are the only one who can reject you. Indeed, it is a wonder the mind can repeat the same familiar projection, even after you have seen through the projection a hundred times or more!

When one believes the mind's projections to be "true," it really does seem like everything is coming from the world outside the self. The mind has been imprinted to believe it is—i.e., *you* are—separate from everybody else it perceives as "out there." Since you are aware enough to recognize you have personal areas that are unclear, you become convinced that everybody else is unclear too. Thus, when you observe others behaving in ways that feel hurtful to you, it is tempting to believe that *they* are unclear. But the fact that you even *perceived* their actions as hurtful comes from your habit of mind. Such is how your mind moves when you experience the energy they appeared to exhibit. Now, in truth, you are perceiving some kind of energy, but instead of accepting your developing thought, you have to challenge your mind and say, "Maybe it's not the way I've seen it. Maybe I have a compulsion to see in the way I have seen previously." Where *is* the insult, or the blame? They reside in your interpretations.

The Long Road to Freedom

The journey, then, is what we could call "the long road to freedom." What are you willing to pay for it? You buy your freedom from suffering with the effort you put into the work. There are many elements in working the spiritual path comparable to achieving goals at a physical level. For example, just because someone has a talent to be on the first string of a football team doesn't ensure his place on the team. One's talent must be accompanied by his willingness to apply himself. Given that one has the talent, the greater part of the task has to do with his willingness to *apply* the talent. If you want to play football, you have to get out on the field and give it your best effort.

The same is true of your spiritual path. You might recall here that old phrase, "Everything has its price." In the long run, the price is not that important, actually. The most important thing to remember and appreciate on a daily basis is the fact that you have the *opportunity* to attain freedom from the bondage of karma. Even if one never learns about karma nor dedicates a lifetime or two to cutting through the mind's tyranny, one still pays for the privilege of life. One pays with the suffering one endures throughout the course of lifetimes. When you can clearly see your options, making a commitment to your enlightenment is the only viable course of action.

It is important that you think about the impact and the power of karma, not just in your own life, but for all beings. Contemplate it carefully, but do not fall into pity for either yourself or others. Let yourself touch with awe the mystery of karma, but let what you observe inspire you to mastery rather than overwhelm you in any way. You might ask yourself repeatedly, "Why might I be in the West this life, where life is relatively easy, when there are so many people in Africa starving or dying of AIDS?" Consider the war-torn regions where for generations one culture has tried to literally erase cultures that are different from its own. Ask, "Why am I not there? Something in my past gave me the ability to see myself living in the West, and because I'm dying, I need to make the most of it."

You know you will die—you just don't know when. Death is "the way of all flesh," isn't it? Turning loose of the cells is a natural process. It is part of life. When you do drop the cells, so to speak, you discover who you are without cells. A hundred years from now, what will be the same for you as now? Your body will obviously not be the same, nor your mind, nor your feelings, and *certainly* not your relationships. Take time to think about these things, to pause and marvel at the wonder of it all. There is tremendous wonder riding on the fact that you could manifest a body that functions reasonably well, that you could find yourself where you could either hold a job working for others, or if you want to be a entrepreneur, you have that possibility as well. You can create the lifestyle of dreams, if you are willing to pay for it. How marvelous is this thing you call a mind!

It is true, however, that some people have the karmic imprint to see only how bad things are for them, no matter how fantastic what they have looks to others—which tells you something about what karma is ripening for them. You may even know some who feel highly victimized by the repeating patterns they experience. Clearly, everyone experiences events that are difficult, even cruel. But not all appear to be victimized by the events in their life. Can you comprehend that even victimization is a trance? This way of seeing is highly creative, however, and replicates itself in experience after experience until the pattern is finally broken.

Perhaps you have known those who have the karmic imprint to see everything as wonderful. This way of seeing can be quite confrontational for those who do not see in the same way, and the temptation to shut down the bliss component of the one who sees blissfully can be very strong: "Everything can't be wonderful—sober up!" For many, seeing through blissful eyes can be a trance of denial—a mental strategy to avoid feeling the suffering that is all around them. Whether they know it or not, they are imitating how the mind perceives the world when the karmic imprints are all erased. It is an imitation, however, for when one sees clearly without the imprints, it is quite likely you will never know what they see, for the need to talk about their experience dissolves as well. As a rule of thumb, remember that what arises in your life has *everything* to do with how you see yourself and how you interpret the energy exchanges between you and your world.

As Karma Dissolves, Purification Practices Become Important

As you begin to dissolve the karmic imprints, several things happen. Some of the mental chatter falls away, and you find that the mind is quieter. You begin to take in the wonder of creation, noticing that the world around you seems to change before your very eyes. What is changing, of course, is your way of seeing. The recognition arises that you must effort to keep the mind pure. Whereas in the past you might have felt controlled by your mind and its trances, as the imprints dissolve, you recognize the importance of controlling your mind. That is, rather than allowing it to run loose—fixating on whatever fantasy or obsession arises in the moment—*you* decide what you want the mind to hold or process.

Movement into this stage of the path allows new appreciation for the powers of the mind. You become highly sensitized to the energy of all the thoughts that pass unbidden through the mind. Those you recognize as unbecoming thoughts may actually cause you pain. At this stage, you literally begin to *feel* their presence, whereas previously you may not have paid much attention to passing thoughts. An aggressive thought arising in a dream can suddenly awaken you with a pounding head or a sharp pain in your abdomen. You learn to guard carefully the precious space of the mind, protecting it from the intense intrusion of thoughts born of destructive energies.

Should an angry or deceptive thought arise about another person, you will, in the moment of its arising, be drawn to do some mental purification. Likely, you would immediately try to see the other as your teacher, or as a Buddha. In your mind's eye, you would bow deeply and reverently to him, showering him with gifts, anointing him with precious oil and waiting on him as if you were the loyal servant. Although this might sound a bit off-putting to the ego, as karma is dissolved, the mind space becomes so precious that no sacrifice of pride is too great to protect it. You will have become much too sensitive to distortional energies to allow any to creep into the temple of the mind. Should you hear someone shouting obscenities in a fit of rage, likely you will purify mind on that person's behalf, as you might also do on behalf of the one who was the recipient of the angry energy.

Purification practices take on new importance as you see the mind differently. You recognize that of the three functions you have to purify (thoughts, speech and actions), the most perilous to you is your thought realm. Because speech and action are always on display, should you suffer an inopportune moment of frustration or irritation with another, the other hears your words. Likely, you will be embarrassed and will apologize immediately, setting aright the inappropriate energy exchange. The same is true of your actions.

Your thoughts, however, are another matter altogether. Because they are kept to yourself, there is no external event that causes you to face up to them or that causes you embarrassment. In fact, because they are internal, you may even indulge them, creating an entire fantasy that contributes nothing of value for yourself or the other. If the thoughts are pure, however, there is little to worry about in the realms of speech and action, since both follow thought.

Every Piece of Karma Is *Just a Thought!*

Although most do not attend much to their thoughts, know that the work of taming the mind both begins and ends in the thought realm. All suffering arises in the mind, and until the tyrannical grip of the mind is softened, one will never realize that one can experience pain without suffering. Pain is a part of life; suffering is what the mind makes of the pain. True, none want pain. However, often it is a gift in disguise, since it forces one to pay attention differently than one did before the pain intruded on the awareness.

As you deepen into the introspective journey to dissolve karma, a most fascinating thought will one day dawn on you. Perhaps you will awaken one morning bursting with the realization that each and every piece of karma is *just a thought!* All the ways you have been hard on yourself or others, all the times you ascribed ulterior motives and meanings to your perceptions, the hatred, anger and/or depression you have felt—all (yes, *all*) are but thoughts you had.

If you think you are ugly or stupid, too fat or too thin, don't believe for a moment there is anything real about those impressions. They are karmic impressions that arise as thoughts—*just thoughts*. You do have a choice: you can reinforce them or you can turn loose of them. Thoughts with strong karmic force will arise most often, and likely you will find that you have to release them many times. All those situations that appear to be manipulating you, controlling you, setting you up for failure or compromising you in any way are rooted in your thought realm. You react to them as if your projected interpretations are real, and you suffer—but for what? All that suffering for mere *movements of your mind!*

Jesus told his disciples, "Be not conformed to your world, but be transformed by the renewing of your minds." Such excellent advice! It matters what you think about; it matters where and how your mind moves. It matters that you "renew" your mind on a daily, hourly, even momentary basis. Such is how you move your identity from the field of karmic repetition into the field of enlightenment. Just as karma emanates from your mind, so does your enlightenment. As the Buddha taught his disciples, the only thing more hidden to the mind than emptiness is karma.

A Visualization for Mind Renewal

I was taught a powerful exercise for mind renewal by my teachers, which I will share here with you. As you awaken each morning, create your first thought like this: "May all beings awaken from the trances that rule their lives." As you sit up, take a few fresh breaths, visualizing on the out breath a dark energy being released with the breath. This is how you release the stale energy that may have accumulated during the night, whether from the lingering energy of a nightmare, or simply from poor air circulation in your bedroom.

Then visualize the five Buddhas or great beings surrounding you, each wearing a robe of bright color (blue, yellow, red, green and white). See their brightly colored robes emanating a light of the same color, which comes to and surrounds you. Begin to breathe in the light from these five colors, but as the light coalesces before you, it blends together and comes in on the breath as pure white light. As you take in the white light, let it fill your head as you hear the sound "Om." Bring the light on your breath down to your throat area, and see it becoming bright red as you hear/think the sound "Ah."

As you release your breath on the exhale, visualize the light on the breath dropping into your heart area and coming out of your heart as a stream of blue light. As you do this, hear/think the sound "Hum." The Om purifies body, the Ah purifies speech and the Hum purifies mind. Repeat the visualization three times. As you see the blue energy coming out of your heart area, think of it as your blessing to the world.

A significant lesson in this visualization is to move the mind from the head to the heart. Most believe the mind to be in the head because that is where the activity of the brain takes place. However, one of the secret (or hidden) teachings of the Buddha was that the proper placement for the mind is in the heart. When you can love with your head and think with your heart, you are beginning to open to your Buddhahood.

4

Karma and the Mind

Building on the foundation we have established as to how karma works, this chapter will address karma in one of its many practical dimensions. When most people think of karma—of those, that is, who *do* think of it—they tend to think of it in one of three ways: something they are trying to dissolve, a personal debt they are trying to repay or as some abstract notion that lacks a functional or practical application. It is important to consider how karma plays out in day-to-day interactions. The real test of one's spiritual development lies not in how many right answers can be proffered, nor in how many books have been read. The real test is in how one lives the teachings or the practical application of wisdom and compassion.

Every activity you touch in life—whether through observation or participation—is brought into consciousness or generated through what we could call a "play" of emptiness and of karma. To be clear on these terms, *karma*, you will recall, is the set way of seeing that one brings into his or her life. The mind, via the ego, seeks to replicate the type of karmic awareness imprinted in the creative process of the individual.

By *emptiness*, we are referring to the true nature of everything. You know from your middle school and high school science classes that even though a brick wall appears solid, even behaves as a solid, its true nature is empty. You learned that at the atomic and subatomic levels, there is literally *many millions* of times more space than there is substance in the atomic configuration of particles that coalesce to compose the brick wall. Thus, early in your education you learned that for the most part, things are not as they appear. In the example of the brick wall, the appearance is very hard and solid. Yet when we penetrate all the way to the core of the matter, we discover that the apparently solid brick wall is mostly space, with an infinitesimally small amount of actual substance.

If you study the mental movements of your fellow humans, you will discover that there exist not only individual projections but collective projections as well. Most people understand karma as simply a debt-oriented system. Indeed, karma does arise to afford opportunities to purify energies of past interactions that were of a distortional nature. Such is an accurate notion at a basic level. Looking more deeply, however, we can see how karma plays out in practical ways and, in so seeing, gain new appreciation for the ways it complicates interactions.

The Play of Karma and Emptiness

We begin by acknowledging that everything arising in awareness does so from an intriguing play of karma and emptiness. Now, at first this "play" is not observable, which is why so few challenge their mental projections with any regularity. In the conventional experience, it just does not occur to most people to ask within, "Why do I have this perception?" Or, "Where does this feeling come from?" Or, "How is it that in my field of experiencing, it looks like this to me?"

For example, imagine that you are driving down the road and someone cuts you off, exhibiting an obscene gesture to you in the process. Your anger flares, and perhaps you rationalize that you haven't done anything to this person. You think, "I don't even know him, and look at how rude he is being." In the face of arising anger, most forget to ask themselves, "Where is this anger coming from?" Even though the anger might appear to be coming from the event, to get to the truth you will have to go deeper. The event itself cannot produce the emotion. The emotion that arises in a person does so in accordance with how such situations in the past have been experienced—how the mind interpreted them, how the mind filed them and how the mind retrieved those files at later dates. In this application, karma and mind are inseparable.

Most people believe that whatever appears in their awareness at a given moment is actually happening in that moment. In fact, most not only believe that everything is actually as it appears, but they also believe they are seeing/perceiving objectively. In truth, people see the world not as it is but as *they are*, or as they are conditioned by karma to see it. If you listen carefully to how people describe what they think they see "out there," you will notice that they are describing themselves, their perceptions and their paradigms. If you disagree with the perceptions they describe, it's likely that they will think there is something wrong with the way in which you see.

As situations arise in awareness, the field you perceive acts as a projection screen, empty of any meaning until mind so designates. The screen allows one who is able to see the interactive exchange of energies, or play of karma and emptiness. The karma part is what is reflected/projected from the past, fed through ego mind. Essence mind, however, is rooted and grounded in the reality of emptiness rather than arising appearances, and it contains the vast field of possibilities awaiting emergence.

Indeed, these two levels of consciousness are exchanging energy all the time. We might say that there is *Consciousness* (the field of perception in which emptiness arises) and there is *consciousness* (where the ego mind functions). Remember, the ego mind will do anything it can to continue the projection and to replicate the pattern of perception. Such is the way ego mind works. Essence mind, on the other hand, is brimming with creative possibilities that karmic ego mind has blocked from awareness. The real question is, "How is it that I participate in these repeating patterns without ever questioning them?" This question is particularly poignant since the point from which the karmic field is driven arises again and again in the exercise of repetition compulsion, or the unconscious compulsion to repeat karmic patterns.

If we can accept the play of emptiness and karma, then every perception, as well as every replication of a past perception, results from emptiness and karma operating on the organs of perception as well as on the activities of perception. Both ego mind and essence mind participate in the moment-to-moment arising of perceptions. One is seated and grounded in emptiness, the other in karma. As perceptions arise, it becomes increasingly important to ask, "Where is this perception coming from?" It is, after all, from a perception that one takes action. Therefore, the greater the degree to which one can identify with emptiness, the greater the possibility to see things as they really are rather than as they appear to be. Inversely, the stronger the identification with ego mind, the stronger will be the delusion, since ego mind is rooted and grounded in karma.

The Value of Direct Experience

In every lifetime, there are multiple encounters with those you have previously known, but not necessarily in the most promising of contexts. Imagine that you meet someone today with whom you share a multi-lifetime pattern of negative experiencing. Even though you are unaware of having any history with this person, the karmic imprint awakens. The part of mind that is seated and grounded in karma recognizes the energy field of the person. Beneath the conscious level, something is familiar.

The karmic seeds begin to grow in the landscape of experiencing, and you find yourself—whether you even know it or not—playing out some kind of repeating pattern with this individual. Perhaps the pattern between the two of you has been going on for lifetimes, and every time you meet this person, there is an exchange of aberrant energy that goes between you. The aberrant energy could manifest as conflict, but it could just as easily manifest as a highly charged sexual attraction. In the latter case, it is the force of the energy that draws the two of you together, creating the possibility to dissolve the karma.

Most recognize that part of maturing spiritually involves cleansing the mind of negative thoughts. This cleansing process begins with learning to work appropriately with the actual thoughts, directly confronting them as they arise. When you develop the ability to stay conscious of your thoughts and thought patterns, you will likely welcome the very thoughts you want to cleanse, for they provide so much useful information. Each time your irritation is triggered and a reactionary thought arises, you can consciously welcome the opportunity to explore your karmic landscape further. When you approach those tender points in your psyche with full awareness, you cannot help but experience compassion. Full awareness mandates the presence of essence mind, which both holds and offers infinite possibilities for healing.

Often spiritual teachers talk about the value of direct experience. When this phrase is used, it becomes immediately clear that the teacher is not talking about ordinary experiences. Direct experiences are those in which essence mind is brought fully to the surface of consciousness. In other words, there is no karma filtering the experience. There is only essence mind holding the field of *Consciousness*. When one is able to generate a direct experience, what arises in one's awareness is a highly engaged, deeply penetrating neutrality. One has the capacity to be fully present, fully engaged, profoundly connected *and* neutral. "Neutrality," as used here, is not an indifferent state, as some might be inclined to believe. Rather it is literally a state of mind wherein there is no ego.

One can begin to understand the importance of these two faculties of mind: the one rooted in emptiness, and the other rooted in karma or ignorance. When the word "ignorance" appears in this context of mind, it is not used to indicate lesser intelligence. Rather it is indicative of being unaware that there is any way to see apart from karmic imprinting, unaware that essence mind even exists, unaware of the true nature of everything (empty).

As you are probably recognizing, most of your interactions with people involve ego mind, viewed and experienced through the lens of karma. When you are looking through the karmic lens, however, you simply cannot have a direct experience of *anything*, let alone a direct experience of emptiness. What is meant by this word "emptiness" is a state of being empty of karmic input, karmic reflection and karmic repetition. "Empty" does not mean there is nothing there; it means you are empty of karmic influence or imprinting. Thus, in touching emptiness, the mind is freed from ego and becomes one with the true nature of everything.

Enlightenment Already Exists in Your Essence Mind

The play of emptiness and karma, then, is responsible for the arising of all perceivable phenomena. Perception is an interesting faculty, requiring both a perceiver and a field of perception. Are these two dependent on one another, or do they exist independently of each other? Which arises first—perceiver or field of perception? If they are indeed separate, one must follow the other, but which? Or perhaps they are not separate, since each must appear in order for the other to appear. Does one generate the other, or do they arise simultaneously? Do phenomena arise first in the field of perception to be noticed by the perceiver, or does the perceiver project phenomena on to the field of perception?

Clearly, ego mind alone cannot venture adroitly into these realms, for projecting mind lacks the ability to enter the mysterious. It is essence mind that enters and contains all mysteries, for essence mind is the palace of the numinous. Ego mind is bound in the conventional reality, but when one seeks to go beyond the conventional level, something vaster is needed. Essence mind—or you could say "wisdom mind"—is the field of *Consciousness* that holds your enlightenment. The good news here is that you do not have to create your enlightenment. In fact, there is no way you could create it. It already exists in essence mind—you merely have to let it shine through!

Eventually, you will become aware of your enlightenment. It usually becomes obvious, although not fully realized, after you have a direct experience of emptiness. Although your enlightenment already exists, it cannot be perceived by ego mind, for it is a profound mystery. The luminous nature of *Consciousness* is incompatible with the lower vibrations of ego mind. As the ego mind begins to dissolve, however, one sees the true nature of all phenomena—which, like essence mind, is empty.

When the ego mind perceives something, its tendency is to cling to the object of perception, holding it as "real." As the ego mind dissolves, however, so do all the "real" phenomena it has thus designated. That which is truly real cannot be rooted nor grounded in karma but is rooted and grounded in wisdom, or emptiness. Whereas essence mind sees accurately what is, ego mind can only replicate the past—its version of reality.

For example, recall a time when you came home from work after having had a difficult day. You may have wanted to rest, but the ego mind wanted to replay every discomforting detail, and you found yourself perhaps reliving the worst moments of the day. Clearly, you did not enjoy the experience, but the ego mind must function this way, re-creating the experience for your internal review, because it is rooted in your karma.

The more you learn to operate in the world with essence mind, the easier it becomes to simply release arising thoughts and images—even the highly charged ones. In the matter exampled above, likely the release would come long before you left the office. Rather than obsessing over what went wrong, you would find a curiosity emerging about the energetic manifestations in your day and would probably ask yourself, "How did this or that arise?" Essence mind, rooted in emptiness, projects no meaning onto any experience and is far too spacious to congeal around energies and interpretations that are not real.

If your investigation of ego mind is to create greater awareness of essence mind, you will undoubtedly find yourself asking again and again, "How is it that my mind made such and such of this experience?" The investigation has a twofold purpose. In the first place, you investigate to expose the projections. Simply stated, it is impossible to consciously dissolve anything you have not clearly seen. In the second place, the deeper part of the investigation is to discover essence mind. The interplay of ego mind and essence mind at a personal level reflects the interplay of karma and emptiness at a much vaster level.

Essence Mind vs. Ego Mind in Relationships

When interacting with others, you will, of course, experience their karma as well as your own. Usually you will discover that they are in your life because their karma and your karma are mutually stimulating, which turns out to be good for both of you. Karma triggering karma will help you become aware of those areas where you have not yet established yourself in essence mind. There is a great benefit in having others show you their karma, which will likely point out some of your own. Although you might at times forget to question your own projections, when you see their projections, your curiosity will be piqued and you will find yourself wondering how it is they are seeing in the ways they appear to be seeing.

Of course, your greatest insights will not dissolve the karmic projections of another person. Indeed, the only perspective you can change is your own. When you find yourself in the position of trying to purify karmic energies from the past with another individual, it is tempting to stay focused on what the other needs to do or change. Clearly, when the karma of another triggers your karma, it can produce conflict in the relationship, which usually brings out old behavior patterns. You see them through your projections and you become pointedly aware that if the other would "just change the tone of voice or that one nitpicky little habit," the relationship would flow much more smoothly. Although it does seem that the two of you are relating to each other, if you are investigating the play of emptiness and karma, sooner or later you will have to deal with the probability that each of you is only relating to your own karmic projections.

In truth, if you want the other to be different, you will have to see her differently. To see the other differently means you will have to *be* different in relationship to her. You must question your own mind to clearly grasp your own projection. "How is it," for example, "that I see her as a nag? How else might I see her?" In very blunt terms, you are how you see. If you see yourself as a thief, you will in fact steal. While such is a statement of the obvious, the same is true of how you see others. How you see another in a given moment is who you are in that moment. When you change how you see the other, you change how you respond to her. It is also true that if you change how you respond to another, you will change how you see her.

Ego mind would have you view others with accusation, whereas essence mind would have you view them with compassion. Whenever you blame others, you are actually admitting your dependence on them. In that moment, you need the other to justify your egoic position: "I'm angry because he insulted me." To say something like this is to actually say, "I need him so that I can have my anger." Likewise, "I'm not loving because my mother didn't love me," really means, "I need my mother so I can continue to be unloving." In truth, the issue—according to essence mind—is not what the other did to you; the real issue is how you choose to respond to the situation. If you choose ego mind, you cannot avoid blaming or accusing. If you choose essence mind, you have the option of compassion.

Essence mind is the source of true self-awareness, the faculty of mind that allows one to stand apart from raw egoic feelings and examine how one sees self and other in the moment. Somewhere between perception and reaction lies one's freedom to decide the outcome of an event. For most people, however, the reaction follows the perception too quickly, with no opportunity for essence mind to offer compassionate awareness. Reinforcing old karmic patterns becomes less what someone "does" to you and more how you respond to what appears to have happened. Since the appearance arises from karmic projection in the first place, you simply cannot trust it as being valid—no matter how strong your feelings are in the moment. If you move immediately from perception to reaction, you have reinforced that old, possibly painful pattern.

Most of the karmic issues you find yourself currently working on go back lifetimes. What may initially arise to wound you in one life gets reinforced perhaps in the following ten lifetimes. Although you cannot remember the original wound—nor the ways in which you reinforced it—you find yourself correcting karmic distortions that might seem to arise in the present life but are actually much older. This is true, of course, not only for yourself but for all those with whom you have contact as well. It is true both for the people with whom you feel closeness and those with whom you feel at odds. Perhaps this is the first time you have had the opportunity to greet them with essence mind. Perhaps this is the first opportunity to put a little distance between your perceptions and your reactions. Perhaps this is the first moment you have been capable of behaving differently so that you can see them differently. What a precious life this is for you!

One of the most beautiful aspects of essence mind is that it holds the vastness to experience the high-functioning interdependence that makes creation work. Consider the universe for a moment. It could not be an organized system of light without the beautiful interdependence existing among all the celestial bodies that together compose the universe. Think how different the universe might appear if all the stars were on ego trips! Some would underutilize their light, others might be aggressive with their light and some might get caught up in competitive brilliance! What would be lost in the madness is the sense of the unified whole—the remarkable quality that defines the universe as you experience it.

Ego mind tends to fixate on self and other. The lowest ego frequency is the fixation on other with accusation and blame: "You made me lie." "She ruined my day." "He took away my chance at something great." "She didn't love me enough." "They betrayed me." As can be readily seen, these are all statements of a highly dependent personality—one that needs others to blame for all the things that are projected to be wrong with the self. As the ego becomes stronger, however, the growth curve is seen in growing reliance on oneself. The dependency on others falls away as one matures spiritually, taking increasingly greater levels of responsibility for how one sees both the self and the world in which all interactions take place.

It is the mature ego, having been polished by the experiential buffeting of lifetimes, which opens to essence and experiences personal identity in the "we." The "we" that composes the Oneness is, of course, too vast to be contained by ego mind. Essence mind, on the other hand, because it is empty of any nature of its own, is vast and inclusive, like the universe. The Oneness is another great mystery— too profound for the grasp of ego mind yet foundational for both the universe and evolving *Consciousness*.

Shifting from the "I/Me" to the "We"

If you study the highest functioning humans gracing Earth at the present moment, you will note that all have, through various means, created the paradigm shift from the "I/me" to the "we." They understand that their personal lives are really not about themselves per se. Without denying the personal level, they are able to see beyond it. The roots of their identity are established in the ground of Oneness, or essence. Whether or not they might use this terminology, they are functionally participating in the play of karma and emptiness.

One of the trappings of the Western world is that Western languages are very egocentric. It is nearly impossible to express an idea or insight without reference to the "I." It is the heavy emphasis on the notion of "I" that creates the strong egos for which Westerners are known around the world. One "I" asserts itself against another "I," which reinforces the sense of self and other. From this juncture, it is not far to the point where one "I" sees itself as better than all those others and the notion of supremacy is born. In earlier tribal societies and *gylantic* societies (those societies that engendered, supported and demonstrated genuine balance in masculine and feminine energies), this "I" notion would have been seen as quite an aberration. In fact, it is the overidentification with "I" and the projection of supremacy that lie at the root of all aggressions.

As you learn to operate more and more from essence mind, you will discover that the compassion you generate is quite surprising. You begin to recognize that the people of your relationships have come to you—whether or not they are aware of the fact—to offer a gift. When ego mind is in charge, it seems like *they* are doing something to *you*. As you grow more and more into essence mind, you see the pain that drives their actions, and you are moved with compassion at the prices all pay to get their lessons. Ego mind—with its justifications, defenses and reactionary flares—can only reinforce the karmic patterns. On the other hand, essence mind—through grace and love—finds ways to dissolve the energy that drove the karmic projections in the first place.

Learning to Look through the Eyes of Essence

Thus you come to understand that in addition to investigating the mind's operations and challenging it at every single step, you must also learn to look through the *eyes of essence* at all beings. This is a learned skill, since all are habituated to see through the eyes of ego. It is a very important skill, however, since you are now practicing seeing like a Buddha. It seems easier to find your Buddha eyes if there are no others around to try your patience or challenge you. However, the truth of the matter is that you need the triggering of your projecting mind so that you can observe whether you look out more through the eyes of the ego or the eyes of essence. You gain the opportunity to reflect upon the emotionally charged moments and wonder, "Did I move more toward emptiness or more toward karma?"

You will recognize your movement toward emptiness/essence as you become less and less reactive in moments where feelings—perhaps strong ones—arise. You ask, "Can I be at peace in this moment without these feelings jerking my chain?" What you discover is that essence mind can be inserted between perception and reaction, generating spaciousness replete with possibilities.

Another signal that you are moving toward essence mind is revealed in the presence of the neutral observer, or the quality of mind (essence mind) that tranquilly observes each moment of arising without placing meaning on it. Essence mind is eternally curious. Thus when you investigate how and why your mind moves in a certain way by inquiring of it, what you are really doing is inviting essence mind to understand ego mind. Such is the way in which you discover the spaciousness between perception and reaction, thereby learning that you need not be controlled by emotional reactivity.

Further, you draw the curiosity of essence mind into your interactions with others such that the observer is always in charge. If someone yells angrily at you, the observer asks, "What is he showing me with his anger?" If someone flatters you, attempting to stroke your ego, the observer asks, "What is she showing me with this flattery?" If someone rejects a gift you offer, the observer asks, "What is this person showing me?" What others show you may be who they are in that particular moment. Do not confuse who they appear to be, however, for who they really are. In other words, what they are showing you is their karma.

If you confuse a person with his or her karma, it is like confusing the driver with the car. Karma, of course, is the driver, not the car. On the highway, you can be quite neutral about a car. However, put a driver in it who is weaving all over the road, taking wild chances, running stoplights and cursing angrily, and suddenly it becomes harder to stay neutral about that car. Even though you realize that the driver, not the car, is the problem, neutrality toward the car may prove to be a difficult accomplishment in the situation. Your interactions with others afford you rich opportunities to learn this lesson: Do not confuse the driver for the car! The driver is karma; the vehicle is just the body-mind affording the karma to arise.

Of course, there are two parts to every interaction. Although you may recognize that whatever another shows you is his karma, the other part of the interaction is your *interpretation* of what the other appears to be showing you. Generally speaking, this part is your karma. For most people and in most situations, rather than two people actually interacting, it is much more accurate to say that karma is meeting karma. If you have ever had an experience where you came away scratching your head about a given exchange, wondering what just took place, you probably witnessed an episode of karma meeting karma. In the conventional reality, it does appear that two individuals had a mutual exchange through conversation and presence. What is far more likely, however, is that you were relating to your karmic projections and the other to his.

In all interactions, assume that your karma is active. Simply doing so will allow for awareness to arise rather than blame, condemnation or conflict. Rather than focusing outward to the other, your attention focuses inward as you ask, "Can I let go of the irritation I am feeling? My heart is beating faster. Can I just be still with the energy to which I am reacting and observe my heart?"

In each "letting go," you open the door to essence mind, which pours into you with great compassion. There is compassion for what you are feeling, and there is compassion for the other, because essence mind knows that she is not showing you her true self. If the other is unaware of how the mind works, she is incapable of anything other than what is coming forth in the moment. The projected trance holds this one completely, and until there is awareness of the pattern, she cannot help but replicate it. With a little more essence mind, something else will arise.

The Potential of Essence Activating Essence

When you attend to what arises in the moment from the perspective of essence mind, it appears quite different from the ego-mind perspective. In every interaction, the potential exists for essence to meet essence. When karma meets karma, the meeting is usually followed by karma *activating* karma. As karma activates karma, tremendous reservoirs of creative energy can be tapped, expressing a wide spectrum of emotional possibilities—anything from intense conflict to intense sexual attraction. Indeed, these are the experiences that have led to the use of the phrase "spice of life." Clearly, these experiences do add interest to interaction possibilities. However, for the most part, these energy surges and releases only reinforce the karmic projection.

Given the power of karma to activate karma—generating the stuff of which books are written and movies made—consider the potential of essence activating essence in those same interactions. If the relational norm were essence meeting and activating essence, a literal wave of enlightenment would be generated that would encompass the world in a very short period of time. For such a luminous moment to arise, there simply must be more essence mind showing up in relational exchanges.

Even for those functioning considerably above the norm in their relationships, it is likely that 70 percent of the relating comes from karma and only 30 percent from essence. From the perspective of conventional reality, such relating would appear almost saintly. Although it is unlikely that anyone will leap from fully ego-based relating to essence-based relating, this is an appropriate time to begin balancing that ratio—aspiring to move nearer the vicinity of 50 percent from each. As this higher relational state is accomplished, you will discover (with great delight) that moving from the 50-50 ration to 30 percent ego and 70 percent essence is actually easier to accomplish than was the 50-50 state.

The most obvious place to begin with such a task is the paradigm shift from the mind of "I" to that of "we." In the first place, recognize that all sentient beings are seeking enlightenment, whether or not they are consciously aware of so doing. Enlightenment is not an "I" endeavor, even though most will experience significant parts of the journey as such. Rather, enlightenment is a "we" creation that involves all sentient beings, right down to the little gopher who digs the hole you step in, turning your ankle. *All sentient beings are seeking enlightenment.* Perhaps you are the most fortunate of all because you have had the good karma to have this truth pointed out to you. Of course, now that you know, you have a greater responsibility—both toward your own enlightenment and toward the facilitation of enlightenment for all beings.

Clarity Is a Gift of Emptiness

Thus, by the power of essence mind, you create the paradigm shift. The "I" is simply too small a container for the vastness of enlightenment. Those of you who have had interactions with realized beings who are still in the flesh have had the opportunity to observe something remarkable. Realized beings are incredibly loving, incredibly supportive people. However, they are usually incredibly direct people as well. Should you lie in some way to one of them, they are likely to tell you they know you are lying. Although they speak with kindness and infinite compassion for your circumstance (ego-mind dominance), they speak the truth. The reason for this forthrightness is that realized beings see how you are hurting yourself by continuing those karmic patterns. To them, the most important element is not their popularity with you or anyone else. Rather, it is that you break the habits of your suffering.

This is true of most realized spiritual teachers. Having seen the emptiness in all things (including karmic projections) and having experienced emptiness directly, clarity arises. Indeed, clarity is a gift of emptiness, for in truth, it can come *only* from emptiness. Thus, in interactions with students, what needs to be said will be said—not from the teacher per se, but from emptiness, which holds the field of all possibilities for enlightenment.

As you mature into your realized self, it is likely that you too will take on a measure of this forthrightness. As you become more established in essence mind, you will lose the egoic charge around the karma of others. You have no egoic need to be the one who "puts them in their places," nor do you retain egoic shyness about speaking the truth. What will emerge is a great sensitivity to the pain you see connected to karma. You will recognize that the other is not in the "we" paradigm and, remembering how painful that is, you will be moved to say whatever will help others break through the old paradigm.

Enlightenment is also a gift of emptiness. As mentioned earlier, you do not have to create or figure out your enlightenment, for it already exists. When essence mind is functioning, you likely have glimpses of it and recognize how close it really is. However, enlightenment is hidden from ego mind, since its basic tendency is to remain in the contracted "I" stance. The notion "*I* want *my* enlightenment" makes no sense at all to essence mind, which bathes in the luminosity of Oneness.

Shakyamuni (Buddha) used to use as an example the story of a person who became enlightened. He would remark about the mystery of enlightenment, saying that the day before enlightenment, the student looked at the world and saw only *samsara* (sorrow, suffering and contentious existence). After enlightenment, the student looked at the world and saw only *nirvana* (the bliss associated with discovering and experiencing the true nature of everything). The student was the same person, so what, Buddha asked, had made the difference? What was true for Buddha's student is also true for you two thousand plus years later. The *only* difference lies in which mind is doing the looking.

5

How Karma Ripens

E ven after accepting the fact that mind is really the source of suffering, it can be difficult to grasp the degree to which this is true. For example, imagine for a moment you are in your car, stopped at a traffic light. The light turns to green, and you are preparing to cross the intersection when someone on your right runs the red light and almost hits you. In such a moment, it is difficult to see that your karma had anything to do with the experience. It *appears* that the whole event is coming from outside of you.

At first glance, it may seem that the incident has everything to do with the other driver's karma and nothing to do with your own karma. Of course, the fact that *you* had the karma to be in the intersection at the time the other driver ran the light does say something. It says that you—not the driver in the car behind you or in front of you, but *you*—had the karma to be in that intersection at the very moment the other driver ran the light. Obviously, if you had the experience, part of the karma that ripened in that moment was yours.

To repeat an old but very important adage: "Things are not as they appear." One of the most critical, if illusive, elements with which you will grapple experientially is learning the magnitude of the power of appearances. When something arises in your field of experiencing, the appearance seems real to the mind. Many times one accepts the appearance without any test for veracity. On some occasions, however, one may test the perception using the five senses. However, those five senses also arise upon your perception of appearances.

The Ripening of Karma

Karma works very much like planting a seed. The seed first comes forth as a little seedling, or sprout. Next, that little sprout will put out a leaf, or cotyledon. The seedling puts forth a stalk, and the stalk develops leaves. The cotyledon falls away, plant leaves begin to grow and the little stalk becomes longer and sturdier. Eventually it will put forth some kind of fruit, and that fruit will grow and ripen. Now, in like context, karma is generally understood to ripen. As it ripens, it brings forth the fruit of the action. Thus, the fruit, or defining event, that ripens may have a life of its own.

As you awaken more fully to the process, you will recognize this element of ripening. You will observe events arising in your life that have an unavoidable feel to them. For example, you might hear yourself saying something to another and at the same time wondering why you are saying what you are saying. In other situations, perhaps you tap the unavoidable quality of the experience after the fact.

One cannot, of course, predict when a piece of karma will ripen. Each karmic event has a ripening point, and when that time comes, nothing can stop it. The best-case scenario is for one to have vigorously investigated the mind—sufficiently enough to allow seeing through the karmic imprint before it actually fully ripens. In this case, one can actually create a change of probable events, although he may not be aware of the shift in possibilities, since he did not actually see the karma ripen.

One fallacy that afflicts many people is to apply a negative judgment to an event or to the self should a certain type of event take place. If one suffers a car accident, or develops a certain disease, or has the tragedy of losing four family members to death in the course of a year, it is tempting to judge the events as bad or the self as bad for experiencing the events. In fact, there are all kinds of well-meaning people who might ask, "What's wrong with you? If all this is happening to you, it must be because of something you are doing." Anyone who thinks along those lines has a gross misunderstanding of karma. Whenever difficult or negative circumstances arise, it is important to say, "Thank you," since such means that some piece of karma is ripening and you have the opportunity to clear it from your creative process.

The Power of Perception

In Western society, many actually think there exists some independent measuring standard by or through which points are awarded in the course of a life. Some ascribe this to God, others to the corporate world, still others to whatever they believe is expected of them. As a result, many folks learn to be "human doings" rather than human beings, often having no sense of what it is to *be*. Rather, they believe they must take solace in what they do. The system within which they do, however, is likely established on competitive standards, which can raise additional problems.

Tremendous levels of frustration can arise for many who actually do attempt to negotiate the social or cultural standards. Perhaps some of the standards apply, but to numbers of creative, gifted, perhaps eccentric people, the cultural norms offer amazingly little in the individual journey. Sometimes the social standards only create boxes or social prisons from which escape seems impossible. As most of you know, not fitting in the accepted box can have certain repercussions in a social structure. From a spiritual perspective, however, the matter may be quite different. One might be learning that he or she cannot be confined in nor defined by society's boxes (or the perception of society's boxes).

Often it is the painful process of defining oneself outside the social box that accounts for the midlife crisis. At this time, many find themselves at odds with their work in the world, recognizing that it no longer serves as a personal defining point. What they seek, of course, is meaningful holy work. "Holy work," as used here, does not mean working in an ashram or spiritual community. The term as I am using it refers to *how* one does whatever one does. Having a holy attitude about one's work is what makes it holy work. One sees the fruits of one's efforts to be a gift to the world: acts of service, offerings of love. One recognizes there is *Someone* or *Something* using his or her body-mind as a way of loving all sentient beings.

Since so many do not have the karma to see themselves and their work in holy terms, a midlife crisis may be needed to interrupt the flow of the karmic projections. How one sees oneself is a direct reflec-

tion of one's karma. The midlife crisis is actually a call to emptiness.
It may begin with a recognition that one's work is not self-nurturing.
Rather than sitting with the understanding that one's job is not nurturing, it is much easier to focus on the job or career as if somehow *it*
is at fault for the vacant feelings one is experiencing. In truth, the
individual is just discovering the true nature of the career—it is
empty, which is why it cannot provide nurturing.

Others experience their crisis in their primary relationships, perhaps judging them as shallow or dysfunctional. Of course, what
might not be readily apparent to the person in relational crisis is the
fact that this kind of crisis is a call to *love more*. Too often people feel
that they are not or have not been loved enough, and at a crisis point,
this perception becomes very dear to the ego, creating a tendency to
obsess upon it. This is the stance of someone who has slipped into a
dependency trance in the very relationship that is blamed for the personal pain. It is as if to say, "I need you to not love me the way I want
to be loved so that I can believe this pain is real."

Again we must return to the premise that what causes the pain is
the karmic way in which one sees oneself and one's experiences. If
the emotions say, "I am the victim here," then some event will arise,
some piece of karma will ripen to reinforce that perception. It is
important in both joyous times and painful times to observe just how
one perceives both the self and the moment. Should a moment of
irritation arise, it is important to acknowledge, "I see myself as irri-
tated right now." If one suffers depression at certain arising circumstances, it is important to acknowledge, "I see myself as depressed
right now." This is being much more truthful than thinking, "I'm
angry," or "I'm depressed."

The self, like every other phenomenon, is innately empty. Therefore,
it cannot be angry or depressed. However, the mind can *perceive* itself
to be any number of descriptions. But because the mind's perception
of itself keeps changing, this proves that none of these perceptions are
actually real. Were they real, they could not change with the circumstances that arise.

What is needed is a way to invest in one's own life stream with a
huge amount of good-natured curiosity. Ask yourself: "Why did I
think that?" You do not have to judge as good or bad any of the
events in your life—simply be curious about them. "How did it come

to be that I think tulips are prettier than daisies? How did that happen?" Refrain from judging either yourself or the flowers, since the judgment will serve neither. If you have a preference between tulips and daisies, you might ask yourself how the preference arose or why you have it. You may be amazed to discover that the answer will tell you something about how you see yourself in the world or how you see yourself as a part of physical reality.

The Influence of Collective Perceptions

You can be sure that how you see yourself is a product of past karma ripening. Your mind is continually projecting, reiterating and reinforcing the past—or what you believe is your past—into the perception of who you appear to be in any given moment or situation. Yet beyond personal projections, there is a vaster field of shared perceptions operating that can be recognized as cocreative, since they arise in and are reinforced by the collective experience. These collective perceptions, or projections, are equally as karmic and equally as creative as your individual projections. They influence your field of experiencing because you have the karma to see yourself living in a time and a place where a group of people see certain appearances in the world similar to the way you see them.

This collective perception arises even if you hold different interpretations of how time influences the experience. Some will tell you that there is neither past nor future. What exists is only the now, and consequently if one perceives himself or herself as living in the fourteenth century, then that person is actually in the fourteenth century. Although this may be a bit simplistic, it is a notion that appears to be borne out by quantum physics.

If you perceive yourself as living in the twenty-first century, it is impossible (or so it appears) to look at the world around you and perceive the fourteenth century. However, what should be remembered about time gradations is that, not only are they arbitrary, but they are karmic in the sense that they are a product of how many times you have seen yourself on this planet. If you have had experiences where you saw yourself in the fourteenth century, then you are not likely to see yourself in the fourteenth century now.

But it is important to realize that such does not mean your projections are necessarily different from what you *designate* to be an earlier time. In other words, there are many people who see themselves in the twenty-first century who are working on issues left over from a time they perceived to be the fourteenth century. Even though they see themselves in the twenty-first century now, they have never managed to extract themselves from the energetic obstacles they perceived in the fourteenth century. Such begs the question, "Are they really living in the twenty-first century, or are they living in the fourteenth century?" If you can at least allow the question, you are not likely to be comforted by the social/cultural box of the twenty-first century Westerner.

Most of your peers will adamantly hold to the notion that this is unequivocally the twenty-first century. However, some of the activities being played out in the twenty-first century arose in the twelfth, fourteenth or the sixteenth centuries—times, most would assert, that were less enlightened than most would claim the twenty-first century to be. Most Americans would adamantly assert that the slave trade ended with the Emancipation Proclamation, but such is not true. Although it may be black market and it may be hidden from public view, there is still a slave trade operating in twenty-first century America. There is a sexual slave trade involving children and women brought from other countries, but there is also an indentured servant trade, which is kept very quiet by those who engage in it. When you consider the fact that a slave trade is still perpetuated, you really must question which century you are in. And . . . how do you know?

"Oh, I have the calendar," you say. Some would make the case that the calendar is but another example of mass hallucination, or at least mass projection. Then there is the matter of which calendar to use. Is the one that measures by the Sun more accurate, or the one that measures by the Moon? The Sun calendar says the length of a year is twelve months, but the Moon calendar says it should be thirteen months. And those are just Western calendars! If you begin to investigate the tenets you hold as lending some credence in your life, you will likely be amazed to see how many (perhaps all) arise from some kind of a mass projection. That being said, it is probably not a good idea to simply throw them all out. Even mass projections hold the potential to point you in the direction of emptiness.

Fullness vs. Emptiness in Western Society

To achieve the experience of emptiness regarding the events of one's life, one must first come to grips with how full some of those events seem. Indeed, it is the apparent fullness that often becomes the point at which one gets stuck. What drives the ego mind is a desire to feel full, which generally amounts to little more than a reaction against emptiness. It is the nature of the untamed or, shall we say, uneducated ego mind to resist essence mind—which, remember, is seated and grounded in emptiness. To that end, often the ego mind fears anything that holds the remotest resemblance to emptiness, and many individuals experience sheer terror when they consider the cosmic void.

Ego mind will try at every turn to persuade one that full is better than empty. If you study the Western world, you will find representations of this belief demonstrated at all levels of functioning. Of course, such is only illustrating the magnitude of the ego investment in Western civilization. What else could account for the prominence of consumerism, materialism, acquisition, separation and domination that assail you on nearly all social fronts?

Because these notions are based on the false premise that things actually exist as they appear (i.e., fullness), they cannot demonstrate reality. What they *can* do, however, is to provide opportunity for much karma to ripen. As unchecked, ego mind is continually pushing toward fullness-based experiences, which forces the personal mantra to become, "More, more, more." Yet as everyone has undoubtedly experienced at one time or another, the "more" ultimately becomes too much. This is true of food, sex and even possessions and experiences. If one persists in the "more, more" adventure, sooner or later that he will find himself suffocating in the object of his desires.

Additionally, the "more, more, more" mentality generates a voracious internal hunger that allows multiple levels of karma to ripen. Indeed, ego mind is never satisfied. No matter how much one feeds it, ego still wants more. This wanting stimulates "comparing mind," and usually no matter how much one has, the focus goes to what is missing—what others have, or appear to have, that the "I" does not have. What a vicious cycle: wanting more, taking more, never enough! Those unaware of the tyranny and manipulation of ego mind cannot help but fall prey to it. Soon everything is seen through the filtering lens of comparing self to others, usually feeling empty—or at least not satiated—of whatever the focus of desire: food, sex, drugs, material possessions, self-esteem, love, creativity, *even* spiritual helpers!

Clearly, this "hungry mind" forces one to remain in the "I" paradigm rather than entering the vaster, ultimately much more comfortable "we" paradigm. If hungry mind persists, the inner focus is to become addicted to the "I" notion, keeping the individual in a very dependent state. Further, one is plagued with a woeful sense of inadequacy because for all the "I"-ness of the stance, the measuring standard is actually placed outside the self and one must continually compare self to others—or to his or her perceptions of others.

Since hungry mind is ego driven by "more, more," the primary feeling state is a kind of artificial emptiness. One may feel empty, but in reality, one is *full* of longing, hunger, dissatisfaction, comparing mind and ultimately deception. Because one *feels* empty, hungry mind attempts to fill up on the experiences that may have been particularly meaningful at one developmental stage or another, replaying again and again in the mind an experience that felt "full" in its moment of arising.

How One Gets Stuck in the Past

Probably everyone indulges to some extent in the recapitulation of the "good old days," which is not necessarily problematic. However, should one become fixated on hungry mind, projecting the "not enough" colorant onto the experience of one's life, the tendency is to literally get stuck in a past moment that seemed full. In this light, a fifty-two-year-old woman who felt she was unappreciated in the corporate world said to her attorney boss, "But you don't understand! I was a cheerleader in high school!" Clearly, that was a point in her life that felt full; perhaps it felt like life simply could not get any better. She was popular, and other students looked to her with a kind of respect she missed in the corporate world. In a large law firm, very few legal secretaries are afforded the status that a cheerleader is afforded in high school. Thus, hungry mind kept remembering the full feeling of that prior experience as a way of invalidating her present adult experience. Comparing mind could not be silenced, and the present moment held none of the glory of former days. Hence, she suffered.

Perhaps you can recall an older gentleman in your own experiential field who, somewhere between the ages of sixty and seventy, repeatedly recounts one of his football games in high school. Perhaps it was the only game in which he scored a critical touchdown. Every Sunday afternoon, as he watches National League football teams, all his football buddies have to hear about that high school football game. In his internal experience, that game was his moment of fullness. Even though he has had countless experiences since that game, comparing mind has never let any other experience come up to the fullness level of that one game. His inner world is congealed around that football game, and for him it has been downhill ever since.

For both individuals mentioned above, suffering is inevitable, for the consciousness of emptiness cannot expand when crammed into the small concrete box of a single experience. For others, the picture may be considerably larger, but the mind still gets stuck in a kind of time warp. Many of those who have been called "the greatest generation" found themselves as young men fighting in World War II. It is clear that the war became the cataclysm that demarcated their whole lives. When interviewed, often these veterans—some of whom are nearing ninety now—are still moved to tears when they discuss standing on the front lines and observing a friend being shot. It seems that for their psyches, time has managed to stand still. Their bodies, however, may tell another story. They have all aged, raised their families and seen countless changes in the world. Even so, it is as if their lives both began and ended with the war.

You may be wondering what causes such a powerful fixation. Clearly, it is not the flow of time, nor is it the calendar. In actuality, these mind states have everything to do with how the individual sees the self and the world. It is a valuable exercise to review one's own life, searching for the points of personal constellation. Where did ego mind begin defining the self? Did it start with a football game? Of course, no matter which point may be determined as the ego origination point, such is not actually the origination point. Ego awareness too is a matter of karma ripening.

In truth, no matter how much you search, you cannot find your beginning without stretching beyond the parameters of the physical world. Time—the factor so important in the ripening of karma—is a phenomenon associated with experiencing on a physical plane. Your planet traveling around the Sun is the means by which time—at least chronos—is delineated. Chronos, however, has less to do with experiencing than you might realize. All have known individuals who at age sixty appear to be forty, or those who at age thirty-five appear to be sixty. Thus, some factor besides the number of days that go by must be working here.

When all contrivances are stripped away, the one thing remaining is consciousness. As one sees himself or herself, so he or she *is*. However strange this may sound, many people do not really *know* how they see themselves. This is one of the reasons that self-help seminars became so popular in the West during the eighties and nineties. Most people know how they want others to see them—competent, confident, self-assured, capable and so on—but they may not experience themselves in that way. Thus, there arises a crisis point where two factions are at war. One is the image presented to the world, and the other is the image one holds of the self.

The result of carrying on with this internal war for numbers of years can be profound. In early adulthood—say, one's twenties—one may appear full of promise, perhaps demonstrating enormous talent. By age fifty, however, the result of the war may be obvious, and this same person might then appear quite neurotic. Confusion is rampant, and the person may still be trying to figure out what to do with his or her life. In this situation, often the person feels victimized by life, not understanding projecting mind nor the ripening process of karma.

The Workings of Karma Are Deeply Hidden

Those whose profession requires listening to the life stories of others can discover a great deal about how karma presents itself differently from person to person. Some report personal scenarios filled with trauma, but they themselves do not appear to be particularly traumatized by their histories. Yet others, having histories that do not appear to fall into the trauma category, may be emotionally crippled by how they perceive their histories. Clearly, it cannot be the events of one's life exclusively that determine an individual's relative level of functioning. Rather, it is how one perceives life events or ascribes meaning to them that creates the outcome.

But since those perceptions were largely formed in prior lifetimes and projected into the current one, sooner or later a question arises as to whether anyone ever *actually* experiences anything. Clearly, nearly everyone *believes* they are having valid in-the-moment experiences. But for most, it is impossible to know unequivocally that one's mind is actually perceiving in the now.

For example, consider a battered child's situation. It would be a distortion to say that a young child creates the battering by "asking for it," as some who batter claim. In every case, there are others holding the field of experiencing for the beatings. Even so, to find oneself in a situation where battery can occur, one had to have the karma to see herself in that situation. That person did not choose the situation so she could be battered. The karma—i.e., to see oneself as a battered child—already existed before the child took birth. It was the karma, or the karmic projection, that found a situation where the karma could ripen. Of course, those who do the beating must have the karma to see themselves as batterers or it would be impossible for them to take on such a role.

Obviously, both parties have some karma that is ripening. However, while this may be true, one should never allow oneself to become calloused to the conditions that bring about great suffering. There are those who view such situations and coldly think or say, "It's *their* karma; I can't be expected to do anything about it." Although we must acknowledge the karma of those directly involved in any such situation, we must also consider the karma of those indirectly involved. The truth is, if you are seeing or experiencing the situation, it is *your* karma too.

Often karma is approached in very simplistic terms. A commonly held belief is that if you kill someone in one life, in the next life that person will kill you. Although that does happen sometimes, this kind of explanation is far too simple. The workings of karma, so it is said, are deeply hidden—more deeply hidden even than the mystery of emptiness. From many lifetimes, creative perceptions are formed that literally have a life of their own. Left to its own devices, karma will create from those perceptions again and again. If one could bring one's mind completely into the present moment, it would be impossible to repeat the past, for there would be no past. Because the creative part of the mind can literally be stuck in another time (or many times simultaneously), past, present and future blur into an amorphous screen on which the projections come to life. Given such, do you think anyone *really* knows what is going on?

Of course, maturation is continually occurring—not just with the psyche and spiritual awareness, but with karma as well. Although most would prefer to sidestep the issue altogether, the very best thing that can happen is for your karma to ripen. As it bears its fruit and you have the rare opportunity to look at it and see it for what it is, then break the pattern and discover yourself without it. To be fortunate enough to observe your karma ripening is a great gift. Everything that happens to you from the time you take birth until the time you negotiate death does so as an opportunity for you to see beyond your karma. Indeed, a large part of the journey is to recognize the preciousness of life—even with the expensive price tags that are sometimes attached to your experiencing.

To the karmic flow, there is little difference in a karmic seed ripening two years after the seed was planted or two million years. Although it may matter to you, it simply does not matter at all to the karma. The important thing to recognize is that there are no failures. However and whenever a seed ripens is how and when it ripens. Indeed, the very notion of "failure" is nothing but a piece of karmic fruit. As such, it can be easily dismissed if you have the karma to see yourself releasing it. If, on the other hand, you have the karma to see yourself as a failure, life will offer you numerous opportunities for that karma to ripen, thus drawing to you experiences that seem to validate the notion. Of course, with each experience there arises yet another opportunity to break the karmic pattern.

Seek to Be in Charge of Your Mind

When looking at yourself in the mirror, you see something that is familiar to you, and the reflection merely reinforces what you already know. The same thing happens with karma. Every time you see an event or circumstance in the way you have previously seen it, what you see is reinforced. But should you suddenly find yourself in a situation where you simply cannot see in the old way, a powerful shift in consciousness is possible. Such is true of any experience that jerks you out of your conditioned way of being.

These experiences are called liminal, or threshold (to borrow a bit from Latin), experiences, since the placement of consciousness finds itself on the threshold between two paradigms rather than in one or the other. It is upon this threshold that real transformation becomes possible, because the experience demands that you pay attention in a heightened way. The very act of bringing greater attention to the present moment necessarily opens the door to a greater abundance of possibilities and opportunities to see both yourself and the arising situation in a new, perhaps freer and less limiting way.

If someone decided to make a movie on a day in your life, what would it look like? Chances are strong that you cannot easily answer that question. Likely, you are so habituated to mindlessly flowing from event to event in your life that you do not know how an objective eye would look upon it with fascination and curiosity. You need the fresh eye of the photographer to follow you around, selecting points of interest for the movie.

There are really very few people who pay attention—as if standing in that creatively powerful liminal space—to the ordinary moments of their lives. Most go through hours, perhaps days, on automatic pilot, and from the standpoint of consciousness, frankly not much is going on. When such is the norm for experiencing, one is simply reinforcing karmic patterns. Like the proverbial rat in the cage, much energy may be spent, but one goes nowhere. Each time a piece of karma ripens, however, a wake-up call is issued from the deeper regions of consciousness and an opportunity is afforded to find that liminal space.

Seek to be in charge of your mind rather than having your mind be in charge of you. Understand the difference between mind (which is constricted, small, narrow, congealed and transient) and consciousness (which is vast, open, spacious and like the sky, containing everything). If you identify with mind, you will repeat and reinforce the very karmic patterns that cause you to suffer. Know that every word you speak—indeed, every thought that goes through your mind—is some kind of a seed. Although you cannot know when, someday that seed will ripen and bear fruit. Pay attention to what you are planting in your garden. Are the thoughts and words you are planting of a vibrational frequency sufficient to ripen into beauty and holiness? Know and appreciate fully the preciousness of your life, for it affords you an opportunity to open to ripening karma.

Find that liminal space—the threshold between who you *think* you are and who you *really* are. In all things, let the past be the past. You can simply step out of the way of those mental projections rather than dragging them from experience to experience or even from lifetime to lifetime. The past will always bring forth fruit. Allow it, knowing there is no need to fight or struggle with what arises. Allow the past to give you input, but do not define yourself by that input.

The Thief and the Monastery: A Gift of Radical Awakening

There is an old story about a thief who visited a monastery to see if there were any items worth stealing. He saw in the meditation hall a beautiful sword inlaid with many jewels and precious metals hanging on the wall. The sword had been given to the monastery as a gift from a rich ruler whose son the abbot had healed. Seeing the great sword, the man whose karma it was to see himself as a thief became obsessed with it. In waking hours, he thought only of stealing the sword. At night he would dream about the respect and prominence that would be his for possessing such an exquisite sword. He came to the monastery each day pretending to meditate so that he could feast his lustful eyes on the object of his desire.

One day the abbot, knowing the heart of the thief, called the man for a private meeting. They met in the meditation hall, where the sword on the wall was prominently displayed. With the sweetest of dispositions, the abbot looked into the eyes of the robber and said, "My son, I would like to give you a special present. This beautiful sword was given to the monastery as a special gift, but since we do not fight here, we shall never use it. Let me give it to you." So saying, the abbot removed the beautiful work of art from the wall and gave it to the man.

The real gift, of course, was not the sword. The true gift was the fact that the abbot literally threw the robber into liminal space. Such made it impossible for the robber to take pleasure in stealing the sword since it was given to him. Receiving the gift, it was impossible to covet the sword. In that moment, the man could no longer see himself as a thief, thus instantly shifting his karma. Karma, you see, can ripen in many ways, and you are most fortunate if you have occasion to present yourself to any teacher who can and will launch you out of your normal mind space into that liminal space.

Radical awakening simply cannot manifest in the confines of mindless drifting from moment to moment. Such is what the thief did. He was consumed by his obsessive fixation on the sword he sought to steal. His mental obsession took up all his internal creative space, and his lustful mind completely overshadowed any reflection of his true nature to which he might have had access. Whether harshly confrontative (as is the case with some spiritual teachers) or quietly, sacredly manipulative (as in the case with the teacher and the thief), it is the mind being thrown off its regular obsessive, mindless course that opens the door to clarity and spontaneous awakening. Of course, there must be a readiness on the student's part to receive the "throwing off" of the mind by the teacher.

As you can likely recognize, this matter is a bit more complicated than simply retaining a teacher to disturb one's mind enough for the lightning flash of creative intuition to occur. Indeed, although it may be the teacher who waits patiently for the proper moment and guides the student to the point where "mind shock" is likely to happen, the greater responsibility lies with the student to receive the gift the teacher is offering. Fortunately for our story, the thief was able to receive the transcendent moment, likely due to his attending meditation and *darshan* (or group teachings) while staging his elaborate plan to steal the sword.

6

Mind as Liberator

In contemplating liberation of the mind (i.e., liberation from suffering), one must face an interesting paradox. Up to this point, we have held that there are two minds: ego mind and essence mind. We have noticed the functions of each and have shown from whence each arises. However, as we move toward liberation, what has been experienced as two must merge into one. Please recall our earlier example of Buddha Shakyamuni's well-known teachings in posing to students the paradox of the mind before enlightenment versus the mind after enlightenment. As the mind opens to enlightenment, it sees the world very differently. In posing the dynamics of the two states of mind, Buddha would say to his students, "Same mind! What is the difference?"

Clearly, the mind is not the same after enlightenment as it was prior to enlightenment. What the Buddha was actually trying to get across to his students was that the mind *feels recognizable* to the individual in the same way after enlightenment as it did prior to enlightenment. In other words, to the person it still feels like "my mind." Thoughts arise in the same way as they did previously, but generally speaking, there are much fewer of them, since the enlightened mind is not driven by karma seeking to ripen.

For the sake of our work here, we shall continue speaking in terms of two minds, but it is important to understand that such might also be thought of as two functions of mind. Seeing these two applications of mind as separate is helpful in learning to discern karma and emptiness. One could say that the mind is but a reflection of the phenomenal world—it arises from the play of karma and emptiness.

By this point in our study, you may understand karma a bit differently than when we began. Hopefully, you are experiencing greater understanding in your relational realm as well. You may be looking at others and your interactions with them differently. As you continue your investigation of karma, there will come a time when you can actually see the karma of another—that is to say, you can see how another's mind moves in a given moment. The interpretation you put on the behaviors of another remains a product of your karma, but you will begin to have flashes where you do see their mind state that both brought forth and interpreted the moment. Eventually, if you persist in your investigation, you will learn to habituate that deeper way of seeing. Until that time, however, you are neither ready nor able to deny the presence and influence of your own karma.

Learning to Look through the Eyes of Essence

In our previous consideration, we have noted two forms of awareness: one is rooted and grounded in karma, the other is rooted and grounded in essence. The point of discernment comes not so much in naming or describing the two but in discerning which is operational at any given moment. Perhaps you have noticed that your ego voice can sound a lot like your essence voice. As you deepen spiritually, the ego voice begins to imitate essence voice. It does so because it is aware that the observer self is seeking to listen more to the essence voice and less to the ego voice. Thus, ego may view imitating essence to be a matter essential to its own survival. It is the task of the observer self to distinguish between ego and essence.

Although we have used the words "essence" and "emptiness," it would be accurate to say that both are synonyms for Spirit. The word "Spirit," however, is subject to wide ranges of interpretation and projection. Many want to personify Spirit, defining it in personal terms, even ascribing a condition of personal ownership—for instance, "*my* spirit." In truth, Spirit is empty, vast, open and luminous. The choice to use "essence" rather than "Spirit" is to avoid such connotations. Some hold that "Spirit" and "soul" are synonymous, whereas others believe "Spirit" and "monad" (or "spark" of the Divine/God) are synonymous. Although the varying definitions for each of these words may provide some overlap, no two of the three words are synonymous. One could, however, say that "Spirit" and "essence" (or "emptiness") are synonymous.

While the use of terminology can provide points of confusion as well as points of clarification, what is important here is to understand the necessity of learning to look through the eyes of essence. The reason, of course, is so that instead of your interactions with others merely being karma meeting karma, more and more of those interactions become essence meeting essence. In this way, each encourages the drawing forth of the enlightenment of the other. Indeed, this is the way relational connections are intended to work, for every person who crosses your path does represent some facet of a Buddha or a Christ. If they do not appear to be such, this is a good indication that you are viewing them from a karmic projection. However, when you begin seeing what is *really* there, you recognize that the Buddha within you sees the Buddha within them.

Karma and Your Death

It is very important to get the seeing corrected, if possible, before you die. Saying such is not to instill fear or panic at the thought of *not* getting it "right" but to point out the value of doing the level of mind investigating we have been addressing all through this work. Know that the state of mind you are holding at the point you exit your body determines your karma for your next life—right up to the point where you next die. There are, of course, permutations on the theme, but it is the state of mind at that critical point when essence is leaving matter that determines who you will be and what you will experience in the next incarnation. The karmic field for the following life is set at the point where most people would recognize you as clinically dead. This is why it is so important to be at peace with your own death. To die in a state of fear or anger sets the karmic patterns you will bear in the following life.

For those who are actively engaged in penetrating ego mind and generating their enlightenment, the point of death can be a point where you see things as they really are—if you are paying attention, that is. If it is possible, try to stay alert through the whole process. To the extent possible, try to see through the eyes of essence so that you not only take advantage of the unique opportunities death provides but you also open your awareness to the possibilities of seeing through the karmic projections as you create your next life. This "seeing through" is an active engagement of mind as liberator.

Although one should not be overly future-oriented, it is worthwhile nevertheless to focus on what you want to create in your next life. To some extent, the lessons you miss in this life are, of course, influential, for they likely will arise in consciousness on your deathbed. This is why it is so important to do the kind of investigation we have been addressing. Learn where you get stuck and where, on the other hand, you sense free flow and creative aliveness. Notice how and when you touch essence and how you distinguish between essence and ego. Such is indeed the noble work of a lifetime.

Facing your own death now is incredibly helpful, for the movement from life to death and the return is played out at so many levels. Even with the flow of your breath, you "inspire," or take life, and "expire," or die. Everything you experience—phases of your life, relationships, careers and so on—has a birth and a death. In fact, your enlightenment is the birth that follows your having died to your karma. Another way to put it is to say that the karma dies. Although that might be literally true, it may not feel like the karma simply passes on. More likely, it will feel like *you* are dying, particularly when you are pushing on that last brick wall.

Dissolving Karmic Projections

Have you considered how you might view people—yourself included—when you are enlightened? You can count on a highly engaged flow of compassion arising each time you experience a being suffering. Should someone try to insult you, you would have an urge to take them in your arms and say, "Why are you doing that to yourself? It pains me so to see you reinforcing your karma." You may feel many things, but you will not feel insulted. In such a case, what you see is what that person is doing to himself. You literally begin to see his karma.

Seeing the karma of another means seeing the way in which the other's mind moves. At the present, you may think you see the way another's mind moves, but likely it is your own projection. You can readily determine your projections, for they nearly always confirm what you already believe. In truth, there are very few authentic thoughts. Most of what goes through your mind are just reflections of past learning, past beliefs or past prejudices. They recur again and again so that you can see what you are trying to dissolve. How else will you generate liberation? When you dissolve the mental projections, only then do you experience liberation or see life with all its energetic power and profound manifestations as it really is.

Dissolving projections causes you to carefully investigate the areas where you put wedges between yourself and others. At times, a wedge may be erected when you do not approve of something the other is doing. At other times, the wedge may be put in place because you want the other to approve of you. Either way, the net effect is getting stuck in a sense of separation, which is a projection that is very prominent in the West today. The separation projection categorically prevents one from abiding in the "we" paradigm, a potentially liberated state.

One of the ways people find each other on this big planet Earth is, of course, through the force of karma. As with magnets and iron filings, an energetic affinity is experienced with those whose karmic imprinting is like your own. These are the ones who see the world similar to the way you do. Those of you who are old enough to remember the events of the sixties and seventies—particularly if you were politically active in those days—may face with some incredulity the fact that there is still racial hatred alive and well in the twenty-first century. With all the lessons that were supposedly learned at that time, how is it that white supremacist groups who espouse Ku Klux Klan values can still be found?

Such groups arise for two reasons. In the first place, the karmic projections were not previously dissolved in the minds of those carrying the hatred. Secondly, these folks manage to find others who hold the same or a similar karmic mindset. Finding each other, they find something familiar. Because the belief structure is so similar, none find the need to challenge another's karmic take on things because they all manage to see in the same way. From the perspective of transformation, nothing is happening. No growth is happening, and no cutting through is possible.

From the perspective of generating liberation, or moving from ego mind to essence mind, clearly you want *something to be going on.* You want those close to you to be "in your face," as the saying goes, persistently. The goal here is not to create conflict, for that would only be another case of karma meeting karma. Rather, as those who care for you arise in your experience—perhaps confronting you—see them as Buddhas, see them as offering you some kind of gift. Although these situations may not be particularly comfortable, you discover that you can liberate yourself from your karma and demonstrate real spiritual maturity.

Clearly, this work requires psychological maturity as well as spiritual maturity. It also requires one to acknowledge that when receiving input from another—particularly if hearing something one doesn't want to hear—the tendency is to listen *through* one's own karmic filter. Remember, ego mind only allows hearing the old projection, no matter what the other is saying or trying to say. It is a profound experience to awaken to the realization that with all the verbiage of countless generations, no one was ever saying anything to anyone else. The vapid prattling of mouth and mind were for the benefit of the self to reflect its own karma.

In the Tibetan language, there is a word for a karmic imprint, the karmic seeds that eventually ripen. They are called *bakchaks*. A *bakchak* is just an imprint—something that is colored into your mind and through which you look at the world. Although you do really experience them, they are not actually real. You can be looking squarely in the face of a *bakchak* and not see it, but you will see everything else through it.

It matters not what the *bakchak* is—anger or guilt, for example—it is experienced as an affliction. The idea is to learn to have a relationship with it, for you can either learn to relate *to* it (in which case it becomes your teacher), or you will relate *from* it to everybody else. In the latter case, of course, you will stay unconscious, continuing the affliction and demonstrating, as with our Klan example above, that nothing is happening. The other side of the coin is to work with the mind's projections until you eventually see through them. When you see through the mind, you see essence sparkling through, alive and aware.

Discovering Oneself beyond Ego Boundaries

Clearly, the job of continually challenging your mind is a full-time occupation. You just keep peeling away at those appearances. You probably recognize by this point in this text (after regular reiteration) that things are generally not as they appear. The search for essence requires you to challenge your *bakchaks* and dissolve all those projections. When you do that, you are liberating the part of mind that can have a direct experience of what is. The direct experience is, of course, an experience in which there is no karma coloring the experience

The direct experience happens in the "we" paradigm, where connection to everything that previously appeared outside the self is palpably connected to the self in the moment. Direct experience arises only beyond, behind, beneath or otherwise outside the ego boundaries. A good beginning point for discovering oneself outside ego boundaries is with a type of meditation or prayer.

Start by asking for the protection of all the enlightened beings and great teachers, but not for yourself. Rather, see yourself as the spokesperson for all levels of sentient or feeling awareness. In the example that follows, when you come to the blank line, insert the name of someone with whom you have unresolved or irresolved issues. Visualize yourself bowing to this individual, along with the others mentioned.

All beings everywhere, come now seeking the protections
of the great teachers and enlightened beings of all times and ages,
of the precious teachings and of _____.
By the power that is generated through the goodness that
we share in our giving and loving, may all beings everywhere
attain enlightenment for the benefit of each other.
We all ask for this, until we become enlightened.

Praying in this way acknowledges one's participation in the flow of universal life rather than the notion that one is separate from any other piece of that universal aliveness. One asks for the protection of the teachers and the teachings, not because these can actually protect one from one's own karma, for indeed they cannot. Rather, praying in this way places one's mind in the proper attitudinal space, which virtually all traditions of spiritual mind training seek to accomplish. Praying in this way places your mind in the Allness and helps you maintain appropriate humility. Appropriate humility is to see oneself not lesser than others, not greater than others, but in respectful relationship with all others.

Egos, particularly Western egos, sometimes have difficulty in asking for help and hold themselves in a prideful stance. The "I" either will not or believes it cannot ask for help. Simply stated, the mind is inappropriately placed in such cases, seeking to hold itself apart from the universal flow. When you see yourself as separate from this flow, the mind is caught in an illusion of the conventional world. The biggest illusion you have to transcend is that you have a body, that you have a mind and that they are really yours.

The next part of the prayer acknowledges that there is power generated in accomplishing kind and generous acts, and that you dedicate that power to aid all beings everywhere in gaining enlightenment. Further, this enlightenment is not sought for the benefit of any single self but for the *cause* of enlightenment, in which all beings participate. After humbling the ego and placing yourself in appropriate, respectful relationship with All That Is (particularly the one you named), you are in the correct frame of mind to pray.

There is more to all this than just saying the prayer, however. Praying should be followed with attempting to see the world from this state of connection. As you look at others, try to reject seeing them as merely an-other person. Have the sense that they are actually part of yourself, perhaps part of your awareness that appears to be learning through a different body at the moment. If you observe someone going through a difficult time, look at him or her with deep compassion, recognizing that part of your awareness is suffering. Be aware that, body to body notwithstanding, it is the *same life force* in each piece that allows consciousness to take physical form, learn and expand.

As you tease the mind in this manner, challenging it to stretch beyond its ego boundaries, you discover a wonderful surprise. Out of the ego box, the mind can glimpse essence. Beautifully enough, when you begin to glimpse essence, everybody else around you gets glimpses of essence as well. A new way of seeing becomes available—which is, in fact, distinctly liberating.

To Know Liberation, One Must Have the Experience

The goal, of course, is to have the direct experience of essence meeting essence in all situations. Some do experience essence meeting essence when they are interacting with their pets but have much more difficulty when they are interacting with other people. Gardeners—

the kind who have plant juice in their veins—see essence on a regular basis when they are working with plants. Watching sprouts break through the soil and open to the warmth of sunshine, observing the growth and celebrating the colors that come with blossoming—these experiences present essence in opulent fashion. Although essence is obvious in these situations, it may not appear so obvious when interacting with other people—particularly those who appear problematic to your projections. Of course, if you could see through your projections, you would discover that there is only essence smiling back at you, meeting itself.

As we have mentioned, you do not have to create your enlightenment. It already exists and possesses an exquisite shining quality. That luminous quality is already attempting to shine through the clouds of karma, but until you liberate the mind from the old ways of seeing, enlightenment may not appear to be so close. Bit by bit, the light of your essence begins to dissolve those karmic imprints and you begin to see in a different way. You begin to not only acknowledge that you are part of a great and vast creative force but you begin to experience it.

When you look out upon another designated piece of consciousness and you begin to really see who they are, not only will you go soft when they hurl an insult at you, but you will go soft if they compliment you. Neither is more significant from your side, because when you are liberated from karmic imprints, you discover that what you have previously perceived as the perceiver (i.e., you) is empty—empty of karma, empty of ego, empty of any nature of its own. Even so, the activity of perception is still present, functioning quite nicely. You are able to perceive the suffering of condensed pieces of consciousness who believe they are separate from everything else. Not only do you see it, you feel the pain that goes with the ego-bound state. The seeing and knowing generates a flow of compassion so vast it can come only from essence.

Of course, it is literally impossible to explain what a profound experience is this liberation from ego mind. To know it, one must have the experience. There will be times when you approach the empty state, coming very close only to get caught in appearances and lose the connection. For example, let's postulate that you are called to be with someone who is suffering from an accident that crushed both legs. There is pain, of course, but the real cause of suffering for the individual comes from the recognition that she will never dance again, which was her livelihood. You arrive with every intention of being fully present and available in deep compassion. However, when you see the mangled legs awaiting amputation, perhaps lying at odd angles to the torso, a projection arises and you believe the person will never dance again. Perhaps without even knowing it, you have reinforced the person's karma and you have left the place of neutral mind from which emptiness was possible. You confused appearance for reality, and what arose was a case of karma reinforcing karma.

Often, when people in the West talk about their karma, they are ashamed of it, particularly if they have accepted the mass projection that one should be perfect. They may agonize over the karmic pieces that are still actively creating in their life experiences and/or relationships. When one complains, "I'm fifty years old and I *still* haven't mastered this piece," that statement actually reinforces the karma. The better route is to observe, analyze and dissolve karma from a neutral standpoint. Rather than feeling or speaking as if you have been singled out to suffer by some cosmic force, realize that contending with karma is a natural experience on the way to enlightenment. If you have had the privilege in this life of finding a spiritual teacher who can point the way to liberation, you are indeed one of the fortunate ones on Earth.

Assume for a moment that you are walking along a city sidewalk and you observe a man running, looking over his shoulder. Ego mind will immediately make up a story based on your previous experiences. Perhaps you draw an interpretation from a TV program you recently watched or from an article you read in a newspaper. Whatever the source, what you see before you appears to fit with what you believed from that source. Perhaps you learned of a man who had robbed a bank. The mind immediately moves to, "Oh, he's robbed a bank." Under examination, it becomes clear that there is no real evidence for making that assumption. The notion simply arose in awareness because of your past experiences. So goes the mind.

However, should you be able in a moment of wisdom to pull back the projection and simply notice that a man is running down the street looking over his shoulder, you are closer to what is really going on—at least in the conventional experience. What ego mind does with the material of perceptions often has no basis in reality at all but merely offers a reiteration of an old imprint. In paying attention to mind, you at least have the opportunity to catch it in the projection, and you inquire, "Why did my mind make up a story that this fellow robbed a bank?" The answer, should one come, will be a karmic product as well, since movement of the mind is karma.

The same mind that generates and holds the karmic projection is the mind that learns to see through the karmic projection. You could say that it is liberating mind that frees ego mind to behold essence mind. It is the relentless questioning of ego mind that affords the discovery of the deeper, perhaps hidden potentials of mind. It is the deeper potentials that allow you to sense and subsequently create liberation from the suffering that so fills ego mind.

Your World Is a Creation of Your Mind

You both create and participate in numerous experiences where it is possible to see what really is—that the world as you experience it is a creation of your mind. Such is difficult to believe until you actually see it. The mind that prevents you from seeing through the projections is not only the mind that projects but it is also the mind that liberates or cuts through the projected "reality." A good exercise to facilitate training the part of mind that will ultimately cut through is to recall the many examples from your past experiences where things were not as they initially seemed—where something seemed one way but actually proved to be another way. Note the way it first appeared, then note the way it really was. Look back to your childhood, and you will find many situations wherein you believed an appearance but later discovered something else. Notice also that matters tend to be simpler in childhood, becoming more complicated as all that reinforced karma reaches adulthood.

Looking back, you discover myriad examples where understanding that things are generally not as they appear might have spared you some difficult, perhaps intense experiencing. Further, you learn that what you did as a child was to make up stories about the things you perceived to be happening to you, not unlike the story we concocted above regarding the man running down the street. Let yourself take the time necessary to see through or transcend the stories of your childhood, for in so doing, you liberate yourself from the bondage of those stories.

You may even come to recognize how the ego has used those stories in self-serving ways ever since. Or you might recognize that you discarded the limitations of the story long ago. Whatever you notice, refrain from reacting emotionally to the insight. Treat the matter with pure curiosity, wondering, "So how did I come to use my old stories in this manner?" or "How is it that I was able to let go of this piece of karma, and how can I apply that skill to other areas now?"

Liberation is a state of mind. Of course, to actually experience liberation, you must be able to see yourself as liberated (or at least be available for the recognition to arise). Know, however, that this condition of liberation is not something that strikes you out of the blue, leaving you with new skills of observation and insight. Although it is true that the liberated state of mind already exists for you, it is also true that you must clear away the blocks that have prevented you from experiencing it. This process is often referred to as "penetrating the veil of illusion."

While it is the mind that clings to the illusions that block access to pure consciousness, it is also the mind that penetrates the veils. Spiritual traditions of all versions have generated practices to facilitate liberation from ego mind. Although the practices may differ, there is a single element that is common to all: dedication to accomplishing the goal. Ego mind is such a wily beast that all who so dedicate themselves discover that managing the mind is a colossal feat. Although cutting through the confines of ego mind is the most important thing one can do, know that so doing will likely require considerable energy and patience. You can, however, count on the fact that the journey will *not* be boring!

The rigors of the path to enlightenment are hardly unknown, having been addressed by so many great spiritual masters. All have cajoled, teased, prodded, chastised, even demanded that their students do the work of liberation. When you consider that all beings have had thousands of lives, collecting projections and incurring karma from each, the picture of what is really going on in any given moment becomes very big. Indeed, cutting through all that karma, as well as the results of all that karma, is the work of lifetimes. That being said, your enlightenment is but a realization away.

7

Working with the Mind

One of the most important elements in dealing with ego mind is to see how it will use the issues of the world around to reveal issues from past experiences. For example, if you are living in a time when there is a war going on, the ego mind takes the cue from the outer experience and internally follows suit, you might say. In a manner reflective of the outer fighting, ego mind will likely present personal issues in such a way that one feels one must fight the issues that arise. If one gives in to the urge to fight, what must arise is an internal conflict pitting self against itself. Clearly, generating a point of split in the psyche is not likely to master the area or issue that has risen to consciousness. Even though it is more difficult to relax into openness when the energy of struggling, fighting and polarization is outwardly present in the society, still, the trick is to go soft rather than fighting with ego mind.

When you consider your points of inner struggle, it is wise to consider them in the context of your time. Careful observation will reveal the degree to which your ego models on the collective expression of the particular time in which you experience. This is one of the ways the ego anchors itself into what you experience as the flow of time. Because you are experiencing in parallel "realities" that may not share the same interpretation of time, the ego uses the collective expression of a given time or age to create context for working out the issues that are triggered by that collective expression.

The Naming of *Samsara*

Know, however, that the conventional reality is always deceptive. Indeed, it cannot be otherwise, for it is based on the deceptive premise that whatever appears is real. What appears is *samsara* (the realm of chaotic confusion, suffering and repetitive patterns), and if accepted as real, it can only replicate itself in more suffering and chaotic cyclic existence. When one cuts through appearances, however, one discovers *nirvana* (or the so-called pure land), which is nothing more than essence meeting essence and the recognition of the divine residing in everything.

Because the conventional reality is deceptive, it cannot function but in support of suffering. Thus, individuals suffer, families suffer, nations suffer—even the world as a whole suffers. This is the way of *samsara*. The problem for the evolving psyche, however, is that the ego mind accepts *samsara* as a viable definition for what it is to be human. Indeed, *samsara* is *really experienced*, because it appears again and again to the ego mind. The powerful appearance of *samsara* has been the primary affliction of the human realm for millennia, even before the Hindu and Buddhist masters named the deceptive conventional reality. Every person existing in the world today should be tremendously grateful that these masters arose and that their wisdom was sufficient to not only see beyond *samsara* but to name it as well.

By naming an experiential state, one has the opportunity to free oneself from the confines of that state. For example, imagine for a moment that you are conversing with a young adolescent who shows a great deal of hostility but is unaware of the name of the mental state from which his experiences are drawn. The youngster's experience is likely to be one of internal discomfort, but without recognizing just what it is that is being expressed, all the youngster has is his discomfort. Taking him aside, perhaps you explain that the behavior he is expressing appears to be pretty hostile, and you give specific examples of behaviors that demonstrate the presence of hostility. As he understands the concept of hostility, he is given the opportunity to choose whether or not he wants to continue with the hostile behavior. Naming empowers the one who names—not only conceptually, but creatively as well. As the experiential box is named, the first real transformational potential arises.

The First Energetic Field: Altruistic Thought

A few hundred years ago, a Buddhist master by the name of Nāgārjuna offered his students profound wisdom teachings. He told them that if they wished to attain unsurpassable enlightenment, there were three fields of energy they must learn to generate in their consciousness. What he meant by this "unsurpassable enlightenment" was the attainment of Buddhahood. At this particular time, it had been discovered that one could become enlightened without necessarily becoming a Buddha. Nāgārjuna was talking about the "full boat," not just seeing emptiness. The highest of all ways, taught Nāgārjuna, is to seek enlightenment not for oneself but for the benefit of all sentient beings.

The first energetic field he talked about was that of *altruistic thought*—which, he said, should be as firm and as stable as a mountain. What Nāgārjuna was addressing is the state of being void of the dualistic notion of separation between self and other. To attain this state, one must confront the ego mind, since it roots in the opposite notion—that self is separate from everything else. Because the physical sense organs generate perceptions in a linear manner, separating the experience of one moment from that of another, the conventional realm gives rise to the notion that self is separate from everything else. Another name for the cultivation of altruistic thought, which may be familiar from reading Buddhist texts, is "generating *bodhichitta*," or generating the desire to dedicate the efforts of one's own enlightenment to the enlightenment of everyone else.

It is interesting to notice just how pronounced the designation of "self and other" is in the West. Numbers of Americans who went to Afghanistan on missions of relief and peace at the beginning of the "Operation: Liberation" war were surprised that the people of Afghanistan opened their arms and their homes to the Americans. In reflecting upon the situation, most of the relief workers felt that the same might not be true in reverse—that Americans at home might not open their arms to relief workers from a country that was also waging war on American soil. Unfortunately, many Americans can only feel patriotic by marking a strong dividing line between "our side" and "their side," which could completely prevent embracing another culture.

The American relief workers were quite surprised by the Afghanis—who, although they may have lacked formal education, were able to see beyond the political distortions of the war. The general outlook of the Afghani people communicated to the Americans something like, "Wars are what governments do. We are not the government; we are people, just like you!" Again, the Americans could not help but reflect on the attitude most had experienced back home—that all who live in Afghanistan must be terrorists, or at least proponents of terrorism. Clearly, beliefs such as this demonstrate a marked dearth of altruism. Yet it is just such beliefs, collectively held, that have instigated the wars of all times.

If you look at the conventional reality into which Jesus came, the picture is not so different in some ways than the conventional reality of today. War was ugly, and the domination theme was abundant. The conquering hero was allowed to drag the body of the enemy's ruler behind his horse through the streets, parading the grisly image of war before all the townspeople. The ruling notion of the day was "might makes right," and most feared the rulers of even their own towns and provinces. It was into this social milieu that Jesus came, and in his most well-known discourse, he stated, "Blessed are the meek." The people of his time literally did not know what to do with this kind of teaching. Blessed are the meek, for they shall inherit the Earth." Such a statement flew in the face of the elite and powerful of the day, for they thought *they* would inherit the Earth. Indeed, if the meek ran the Earth, it would be a vastly different place. The notion that the Earth belongs to the conqueror is but a product of linear ego mind. Essence mind, however, is tied neither to the linear nor the logical. The vast possibilities that essence mind holds cannot be confined to such finite constructs.

Perhaps the greatest impediment to altruistic thought is the perception of threat. If one feels threatened by the presence of the perceived "other" (or "enemy"), one is confined to linear ego mind, imprisoned in the "I" paradigm. Yet since it is from this very state that one seeks liberation, it becomes clear that this is the state from which it is most important to generate altruistic thought. From the most "en-darkened" corner within the threatened psyche, one can earnestly seek to create an enlightened world for the benefit of all beings at all levels of awareness. Such is precisely what Nāgārjuna had in mind. It is something like children giving away marbles: It is easy to give a marble to a friend who has none when one's own pockets are full of marbles. However, it is quite another thing to give a marble when in one's pocket there is only one marble.

The Second Energy Field: All-Embracing Compassion

The second energetic field about which Nāgārjuna taught was *all-embracing compassion*. If truly embodied, all-embracing compassion would allow others to have their experiences, even if ego mind perceives that you are the target of another's learning experience. Holding the field of all-embracing compassion means that you can see the suffering the other is experiencing before noticing your own suffering.

Unfortunately, most people are out of touch with their own suffering, rendering them unable to be fully sensitive to the suffering of others. Were you to ask people to speak to suffering, they might say, "Well, I don't suffer that much. Life is pretty good for me." Of course, they speak inaccurately. All suffer, whether from the flu, perhaps a broken bone, the loss of a loved one, the loss of a job, failed dreams of one kind or another, or even on what is called a "bad hair day." Most are quite skilled at denying their pain unless it arises from what is considered a big event. The denial is but an avoidant coping strategy, used to get them through the moment of suffering.

All-embracing compassion is, of course, an experiential field that is carried with an individual at all times. This means that the compassion is not directional (from self to another) but is a state of consciousness that extends equally to all beings, including oneself. As such, its presence affords solid moral conduct, which is continually subject to deeper and deeper investigation.

For example, most spiritual traditions teach against killing. At the more basic application of the moral code against killing, some would believe it merely means not killing other people. But if compassion is truly all-embracing, one's personal investigation might take one to the more subtle levels of killing, asking, "Have I ever killed someone else's joy?" Remembering what it may have felt like to have had the experience of another killing your joy, you can readily see such as a viable example of killing, although no person or animal loses its life. To move even more deeply, one might ask, "Have I killed myself in some small way by demeaning myself in a moment of intensity?" Or, "Have I killed another's good name or reputation in a moment of defensiveness or anger?"

All-embracing compassion excludes all killing—even if what is being killed is fairly ephemeral, such as joy or time. The compassion which Nāgārjuna addressed is so pervasive as to soften everything, even the perception of failure regarding one's own goodness. The notion of loving oneself can be fraught with complication, since people often confuse self-love with self-indulgence. Perhaps to counter discouragement or depression, an individual will engage in what has been called retail therapy, or buying things for oneself in an effort to bribe the ego out of its dark emotional state. If this strategy works at all, the results can only be short-lived, for the ego's nature is to be demanding, and it can never, in fact, be satisfied.

The real tragedy here, however, lies in the fact that while the person feels he or she is generating an act of love, such is only an act of self-indulgence. What gets indulged is the part of the ego that imparts the notion that the self is not good enough, or not smart enough, or not *something* enough. When clarity dawns, one can see that such egoic manipulation is simply an avoidance strategy wherein one self-indulges rather that sitting with the pain and going soft around the feeling of that pain.

All-embracing compassion will not allow this confusion of self-love and self-indulgence, but it will afford one to be present and compassionate for the moments wherein she falls from being her best self. The higher the level of compassion, the more it asks of the individual. Of course, this is similar to being in the presence of a highly evolved teacher. A Buddha, for example, does not shake a finger at someone, saying, "Shame on you!" Rather, a Buddha simply surrounds the person with wisdom and love, which is palpable to the recipient, and generally causes him to *want* to be his very best self. In fact, the compassion about which Nāgārjuna was speaking is the antidote to judging mind, because when the field is vast enough, it simply embraces the judgment in such a way that it must dissolve into something else.

In times of war, for example, people carry much more tightness and tension in their bodies than in times of peace. This is true even if one is not actually in the war zone. Just from hearing about the war on a news program or in printed media, a tension arises in the body that often finds its way into relationships of one kind or another. The tension is so uncomfortable that one feels a tremendous need to release it, and often such happens in the relationships that are the closest. As the tension moves, it may take many forms, ranging from out-and-out anger to a kind of overwhelmed stupor. Either way, effective relationship becomes difficult, often stimulating interactions of conflict.

The great masters of the East taught their disciples to see negative mental states as personal afflictions. In such case, one has no need to justify or defend them. Rather, one should do as would be appropriate for a physical affliction—such as go to one who can help you heal from the condition. As you likely know, the ego is not inclined to ask for help, for to do such is to give up some of its perceived control. However, since the patterns that cause the suffering in the first place are often energy aberrations carried from many lifetimes, how is it the ego convinces you that you can heal the affliction all on your own?

For many Westerners, confronting ego mind can be so threatening that they will leave a spiritual path prematurely and seek out another path. When the work becomes challenging to the ego, the tendency is to lose heart in the path and divert to a path that appears easier: "Oh, they *dance* over there; I'll change to that path." True, dancing can be a powerful spiritual vehicle, but all too often, these persons dance until they know all the steps, and if such didn't provide the breakthrough sought, they move to another spiritual path because, "They have *visions* over there!"

When the path becomes confrontative to the ego, rather than reacting to a perceived threat, the better application is to summon compassion for the whole process. Confronting ego mind may not be fun, but it is necessary to discover essence mind. Have compassion for yourself. Have compassion for the levels of resistance that arise, for doubting mind (should it arise) and for the part of ego mind that wants to deny there is a problem. In so doing, be careful not to confuse compassion with self-pity—another state of ego mind that must be transcended.

Transcendent Wisdom: The Third Energetic Field

The third energetic field that Nāgārjuna taught his students to generate was the field of *transcendent wisdom*. By the term "transcendent,"

Nāgārjuna was speaking of wisdom so discerning as to be utterly free of the notion of duality. For most, cutting through the notion that self is separate from everything else is a rigorous task. Before the collapse of the bicameral mind and the rise of self-consciousness, people experienced themselves as part of a greater unit rather than an individuated self. The identity was placed on the clan or tribe, and one could not be whole without the rest of the tribe.

To some extent, the vestiges of this way of seeing can still be found in indigenous people around the world. Some of the great athletes who come to the West from African villages demonstrate this phenomenon in a striking way. Perhaps a young man is very good at basketball and comes to America to play the sport, hoping to earn much-needed money to send back home to the village. However, it is not long before the strangeness of the new country creates within him a deep loneliness, for he experiences no community, no sense of "we," except perhaps on the basketball court. To make good in his new land, he must learn to be an "I," a concept that might not have much meaning for him. True, he finds people with whom he can share moments but none with whom he can share personal identity. Learning to sleep in a room by himself can be an excruciating test, for he wonders how anybody could go to sleep without hearing the comforting sound of others breathing in the night.

The same can be seen for the aboriginal people, as applies to their being "liberated," "acculturated" and "gentrified." To these individuals who still retain identity in the clan, entering the Western world feels very cold and isolated, not to mention unnatural. In truth, the "I" awareness—pushed, that is, to the extremes seen in the West—is a fairly recent newcomer to the human experience. Because it is rooted in ego mind and arises from mental projection, the notion is of course void of any ultimate reality.

Another example can be found in the Celtic social order, with its deep connection to nature, the turn of the seasons and the path of the Sun and stars as related to Earth. The field of experiencing involved a much larger scheme than most twenty-first century Westerners can hold. Living in nature, they saw themselves as a part of nature, not separate from it. Sitting under the stars at night, they taught their children (who were seen as children of the clan) of their relationship to the Sun, the Moon and the seasons. Today, these relationships are not only unacknowledged, but they are for the most part actually seen as "other." Yet in truth, you are so intimately related to the Sun, it literally *cannot* be "other." Every time you eat something from a plant source, you are eating stored sunshine. From the very fact that you eat, you too are stored sunshine. Your connection to the Sun is direct and uniquely intimate. How is it that such a profound and obvious truth got lost in the rise of civilization?

Nāgārjuna's transcendent wisdom is not only rooted in emptiness (the true nature of everything), it is the profound realization of emptiness. From Nāgārjuna's perspective, ignorance (the inability to know the true nature of all things) is but the unawareness of emptiness that creates and perpetuates the illusion of duality. Even such things as your arising thoughts and feelings cannot really be said to be "yours." They do appear to be yours, but they simply cannot be, since most arise as projections from your past.

When projecting mind is dissolved, where will all your thoughts and feelings be? Vast awareness will be available to you, but it will not arise in such a way as to feel like "you" are thinking and/or feeling. You may remember the instance where the Buddha cautioned his students not to confuse the Moon with the finger pointing to the Moon. Although it is obvious that the Moon and the finger that points to it are not the same thing, when there is a fixation on "I," the attention can go to the "I" who is pointing rather than just experiencing the Moon.

If you continue to investigate the mind, little by little you come to have experiences that in fact demonstrate that your experiential "reality" is not real at all. Clearly, you do experience it at a conventional level, but you also see that the conventionally agreed-upon reality is a deception, or an illusion. You find yourself experiencing in a conventional reality fraught with predicaments that perhaps make you feel very small by comparison. Ego mind convinces you that you are not up to the work before you, and perhaps you collapse in a moment of despair.

When you feel overwhelmed by the magnitude of *samsara*, it is good to return to the basics, for they ground you in a way that is productive to solid spiritual growth. Recall that everyone suffers—everyone! They do so because ego mind is attached to certain outcomes that often do not appear to manifest. Perhaps they are attached to certain other people and they lose the connection through death or separation. The other side of the attachment coin is aversion—which although it may feel different than desire, is no less attached to outcome. The events to which one has aversion manage to happen anyway, giving more cause for suffering.

In the face of all the suffering ego mind creates, it is beneficial to recall that there is also an end to suffering. As ego mind is transcended, it no longer holds the karmic seeds that generate suffering. Of course, the path the Eastern masters taught to end suffering was training the mind through meditation and the conscious cultivation of wisdom and compassion.

Practice Generating These Energies

Although this may sound very basic, the judicious application of these avenues turn out to be the proper vehicles for grounding oneself solidly enough to do the work of cutting through the illusion of duality. The basic tenets of unsurpassed enlightenment are but three things: altruistic thought, all-embracing compassion and transcendent wisdom. In truth, if you simply begin thinking about these, you will generate the energy fields about which Nāgārjuna taught. But more importantly, you begin to change. You begin to break through the obvious level of conventional notions, and you find deeper and deeper levels of what it may mean, say, to refrain from killing. You also come to realize the preciousness of such things as the literal terrestrial space you require (and perhaps take for granted), as well as the resources you consume. Likely, you will choose to live your life in such a way as to be worthy of both. You will realize that in being human, you require physical, emotional and mental space, and as you study the mystery and precious nature of each of these spaces, you will awaken to a supreme desire to fill all with altruistic thought, all-embracing compassion and transcendent wisdom.

As you learn to cultivate these qualities, they become an intimate part of you—much like your breath. Then, should you have a day where for whatever reason you are unable to touch altruistic thought, you will literally feel sick because you recognize that such thought is the original state for what you now call "mind." Any of these three attributes is capable of turning your inner world upside down, because each, by its very frequency, presents a challenge to ego mind.

All-embracing compassion will reveal to you the damaging results of experiencing a moment of ill will toward another, or the precious but wasted energy expended on idle or useless talk, or the fracturing of relationship caused by harsh words. All-embracing compassion dissolves ego states that have the potential to reinforce karmic projections.

A good way to practice generating these energies is to begin dedicating your personal efforts each day to one of them. Perhaps you arise on a Monday and dedicate that day to altruistic thought. Keep your dedication before you all day, reminding yourself often that such is what you are cultivating today. Watch your mind carefully, noticing each thought. Should a thought pass through your awareness that does not support the qualities of altruistic thought, immediately exchange it for one that does. It is a good idea to carry a little notebook wherein you can jot down some notes when your thoughts surprise you in a positive way. Also note any areas that repeatedly arise where ego mind resists altruistic thoughts. In this way, you bring to consciousness the more hidden levels of ego mind.

Then, on the following day, dedicate Tuesday to all-embracing compassion. Repeat the process of keeping your dedication before you the entire day. Again, study the thoughts that arise in your mind, noticing those that are compassionate and those that miss the mark. Assume an internal stance that is curious, not judgmental: "Why is it that I was able to move toward one situation with compassion and found it difficult to do the same in another situation?" Keep your notebook with you so you can jot down both the areas where compassion arose easily, seemingly on its own, and the areas where you had to ask it to arise, perhaps replacing some other kind of thought.

On Wednesday, make your dedication to transcendent wisdom. You will note that the work of the third day is a bit different than that of the two preceding days. Today, you watch the thoughts as they arise, paying particular attention to any that pique an emotional response of any kind, positive or negative. Then you ask within, "How is the situation (that seemed to cause this emotion to arise) empty?" It is important to record your reflections, for over time they will prove very instructive. Should you note an event where you have a desire for a certain outcome, ask, "How is the outcome I desire empty?" With this type of questioning, you may notice that an answer is not always forthcoming. However, you will soon discover that the answer is less important than whether or not you remembered to ask the question.

On the fourth day, return to a dedication to practice altruistic thought. Continue rotating your focus through these three, and begin to observe the changes you see and feel in your life. If you are like most people, at first it is difficult to watch all your thoughts as you go through your normal day. With time and practice, however, you will discover that you can "turn on" the observer in essence mind and sustain both the focus needed for your normal activities as well as ongoing and immediate access to all your thoughts. Try this for the space of a month, and be amazed at what happens for you. You will discover that ego mind quite naturally takes a back seat, and essence mind comes forward with remarkable possibilities that you may never have dreamed possible in so short a time frame.

Giving your full consciousness to the object of your work is critically important. All too often, aspirants forget that the spiritual work must be done every day. This work is most productive if it can be done during your normal focus in the world as well as in your meditation time. Such demonstrates that you are not torn between identities (i.e., the spiritual person and the secular person) but that you fully understand the importance of integrating your true self into all aspects of your life. Above all, resolve not to struggle with the work. Be open and curious to the levels that are easy for you, as well as those that require more mindfulness. Your journey is precious—celebrate it well!

8

From Emotional Reactivity to Enlightenment

At this point in time—which is only a few years into the twenty-first century—taking stock of the conventional reality confronts one with displays of chaos, confusion, greed, hatred, anger and attempts by one group or another to dominate some other group. One does not have to be particularly wise to see that the emotional body of Earth is being stretched unmercifully as the planet's populace works out its collective karma. Because each single individual is a microcosmic representation of the planetary process, then as Earth's emotional body is stressed, so too are the emotional bodies of each person experiencing on Earth.

Although the emotional struggles of a given time seem unique unto the time, human nature remains much as it has always been. While the toys and fashions differ from age to age, the human psyche suffers in much the same way it always has and the matter of spiritual liberation remains the ageless order of the day. The ancient King Solomon was said to have remarked that in searching the world over, he found "nothing new under the Sun." His point was that the issues that cause human suffering are basically all the same, age to age, region to region.

Arjuna and Gandhi, and the Call to Duty

The story of Arjuna in the Bhagavad-Gita is literally the story of every person who struggles with emotional balance. He lives in a time of chaos and war. And worst of all, Arjuna, who hates war, is being asked by his spiritual teacher, Krishna, to go to war. Arjuna's family had been the rightful holders of the throne, but Arjuna's father (the king) had been tricked by his own less-than-honorable brothers to wager the throne in a gambling exercise. Losing the kingdom to the relatives, the king and queen were killed, and the children of the royal marriage were cast into the forest to fend for themselves. To everyone's amazement, Arjuna and his brothers were not killed by wild animals but lived innocently and peaceably among them.

When the boys are grown, Lord Krishna appears to Arjuna, telling him that since he has come of age, he and his brothers must fight the uncles and cousins to reclaim the throne as the rightful family. Lord Krishna reminds Arjuna that he has a responsibility not only to his forebears but to those who come after him as well. Arjuna tries to convince Lord Krishna to get someone else for the job, confessing that he knows nothing about fighting, nor does he have any desire to learn! To Arjuna's protestations, Lord Krishna's famous words ring out, "Get up and do your duty!" In fact, the story in the Bhagavad-Gita is the story of the spiritual awakening of Arjuna through his learning to do his duty.

As the first chapter of the Bhagavad-Gita closes, Arjuna has seen the mighty armies of his uncles and cousins, the Pandhavas, and is realizing the magnitude of the situation. He feels trapped. He does not want to engage in warfare and can hardly bear the fact that he is being asked to kill his own relatives, no matter what their behavior to his own family has been. On the other hand, when Lord Krishna personally calls to lay out the plan of his destiny, Arjuna cannot exactly refuse him either. He does, however, offer significant protestations to Lord Krishna about his lack of skill, knowledge and desire to fight. Lord Krishna had offered to both Arjuna and the Pandhavas (Arjuna's enemy relatives) the same options: they could choose to have his armies, or they could have his counsel. The Pandhavas, of course, immediately took the offer of Krishna's armies. Arjuna, because of his absolute lack of experience, decided he would not know how to use Krishna's armies if they were under his control, so he chose to have Krishna as his adviser and charioteer.

Thus Lord Krishna shows Arjuna the entire regalia of the great armies he must fight with his brothers. Taking it all in, Arjuna thinks this is the most hopeless situation imaginable, and he becomes overwhelmed and despondent. He confides in Krishna that he thinks the better option is for him to go out on the battlefield unarmed and simply allow the Pandhavas to kill him. Arjuna is so upset that he throws down his bow and arrows, sits down on the chariot and, putting his head in his hands, gives in to his grief.

Lord Krishna turns to Arjuna, seeing his emotional state, and chastises him for his "impurities," by which he means Arjuna's emotional reactions. In truth, Arjuna is pouting, crying and stomping around, and Krishna informs him that such a reaction is not befitting a man "who knows the value of life." He explains that the emotions would not elevate Arjuna to a higher plane but are quite degrading of his true self (2.2). He begs Arjuna not to give in to the emotional turmoil, calling such a "degrading impotence." Rather, Krishna urges him to arise and become his true self (2.3)!

Clearly, Arjuna does not want to face either his destiny or his duty. More protestations follow as Arjuna lectures Krishna, reminding him that one goes to the hell realms for killing. Of course, Arjuna is terrified, and as many do in the face of fear, he diverts his focus from fear to blame—accusing his teacher of manipulation, blaming him for the suffering Arjuna experiences. Krishna again asks Arjuna to arise in his true nature rather than as this emotional mess.

The story of Arjuna often falls upon dull ears for many spiritual aspirants today, for they see themselves as having evolved spiritually to the point where the mere consideration of war is abhorrent. Thus, great aversion might arise in the mind, resulting from some application of comparing mind. One might ask, "How could a spiritual teacher of Lord Krishna's level demand that his student/disciple actually engage in killing as spiritual duty? There is nothing about killing that fits into the paradigm of spirituality!"

This same inquiring seeker might point to the example of a holy man such as Gandhi, citing the relative merits of the pacifist's mindset to the world at large over those of the activist warrior. Of course, in acknowledging the power of Gandhi's presence in the world, we must also recall that Gandhi always carried with him the Bhagavad-Gita, reading from it continually, particularly when he felt his own emotional nature pulling him to retire his mission. Gandhi saw himself as a modern-day Arjuna, often referring to both himself and Arjuna as "reluctant warriors."

At first glance, the duty required of Arjuna may appear quite different from that of Gandhi. However, upon closer investigation, one can also see how they are the same. It can be a mistake to conclude that what might be required of one in service to one's spiritual duty would necessarily appear only grand and noble. Indeed, Gandhi did not feel that way about his plight when he quite literally felt the presence of Lord Krishna speaking to him and, as in Arjuna's case, demanding he get up and do his duty.

From the position of hindsight it may readily appear that Gandhi's resistance movement turned out as a mission of peace. However, Gandhi certainly had no way of ascertaining such would be the case when he received the call, so to speak. He feared he would bear responsibility for the death of many of his countrymen and had no way of seeing that his efforts would bring about any significant change for India. Indeed, he was fairly sure he would be killed and worried about all the others who might be killed. He wrestled ardently with all the internal emotional demons that arose to subvert both his integrity and his mission. Remember, taking on the entire British Empire is tantamount to declaring war on Britain. To Gandhi, it certainly felt as if he were being called by Lord Krishna to "gird up his loins" and go to war. Indeed, he felt the presence of "death by the sword" to be his constant companion.

Gandhi, like spiritual aspirants today, had to face his own aversion to killing and war in order to fulfill his duty. Thus, there is little wonder at the fact that he took strength and inspiration from Arjuna's story. Indeed, without Arjuna's example, there is little likelihood that Gandhi could or would have accomplished his mission.

Duty Is the Vehicle to Liberation

In many ways, what Arjuna and Gandhi were called to do is not so different from what all spiritual aspirants must do. As one matures, one must put away the emotional levels that could cause one to slip into hatred, greed or despair. Like Arjuna or Gandhi, each must arise and do his or her duty. These two figures, great in different ways and different times, stand as powerful examples for the spiritual aspirant today and perhaps help modern seekers determine that when called to action by the spiritual plane, it is folly to resist or try to foil the plan. Indeed, the battle of life goes on irrespective of whether or not one *wants* to engage in it. Likely, both Arjuna and Krishna would find humorous the notions of many present-day aspirants that they somehow know more of what is needed for the process of Earth's enlightenment than do the great teachers, such as Lord Krishna!

Of course, Arjuna had his moment with Krishna when he threw his big temper tantrum. Following that, his next tactic was to plead with Krishna, claiming himself to be out of sorts, confused about what this notion of "duty" is as well as how he is to carry it out. Like students of today, he begs the teacher to make his decision for him— to just *tell* him what to do.

Lord Krishna, however, is very poised and tells Arjuna that while his words sound very impressive, he is mourning over something not worthy of his grief. He informs Arjuna that the wise do not lament for either the living or the dead, for, "Never was there a time when I did not exist, nor you, nor all these kings; nor in the future shall any of us cease to be" (2.12). Krishna reminds Arjuna of all the changes that one undergoes in the course of a life. Starting as an infant, one moves through the stages of youth, adulthood, old age and death. But nothing ends with death, for the soul then extends its awareness into another incarnation.

He reminds Arjuna not to be overwhelmed by the changes in his own life that he must face, for such is life. Indeed, one should cling neither to the happy moments nor the unhappy moments, for in due course they, like the seasons, appear and disappear. The mature individual simply learns to tolerate the changes without inner disturbance, for only those who can master inner calm in the face of life's changes are suitable candidates for liberation. Although the body is destructible, Krishna teaches, that which dwells in the body is indestructible, and he who thinks that the living entity is the slayer or that the entity is slain does not understand. One who is in knowledge knows that the self slays not, nor is slain.

While this text may trigger aversion in some, it actually does not encourage killing. The same Vedic tradition that begat the Bhagavad-Gita also clearly instructs against doing violence to any living being. One of the greatest paradoxes to confront any student of spiritual mysteries arises in the acceptance of the place of violence within a strictly nonviolent tradition. Of course, to get lost in the relative rightness or wrongness of the text is to miss the point altogether.

Even though the setting for the text is on the battlefield—where the possibility for death and destruction do loom large—the text itself is not about doing bloody battle. It is rather about facing the fact that one must accept one's duty, pay the price or ransom, so to speak, for one's liberation from the prison of suffering.

In that light, the text also addresses emotional obscurations that are likely to arise as each is confronted with his or her spiritual duty. Many spiritual aspirants in the West are offended by the word "duty," feeling that it somehow negates the notion of free will that so many hold dear. Gandhi, however, certainly did not feel as if he had free will in the matter of his spiritual mission—nor, for that matter, did he believe he *should* have had free will. When one becomes mature enough to fully understand the true nature and power of suffering in the lives and creative domains of all beings, one then recognizes that duty is the vehicle of liberation.

Like Arjuna, you took birth to discover liberation. Also like Arjuna, it is likely that what prevents your attainment of the goal has strong roots planted deeply in the emotional body. Arising emotions can be very compelling, and if allowed to hoard too much internal space or focus, they obscure clear sight of the goal, which is liberation. Krishna notes for Arjuna that his emotions throw him out of balance and urges him to free his focus from them that he might once again see the world objectively rather than only subjectively.

Negotiating the Emotional Terrain

Although you might not find yourself facing the imminent catastrophe that Arjuna thought he was facing, the emotional surges that steal your equanimity are no less significant. When powerful emotions arise, the temptation is to get lost in them, believing they are real. To do so, however, robs you of your relationship to emptiness, for the force of strong emotions demands your full focus. The pertinent question becomes, "How does one achieve emotional balance when strong emotions arise to dominate the moment?"

In his pain, Arjuna did what many people do today: he dropped his inhibitions and allowed his emotional impulses to drive him. While such is a popular strategy with many even today, it cannot ultimately be successful for anyone, because it enslaves one to an emotional pendulum, yanking one back and forth with the emotional flow of the moment. Many people think that the only way to express their emotions is to act out, or direct their feelings *at* someone else. In truth, outward expression of one's feelings should be for the benefit of oneself, not some other individual who might get caught in the wake of an overpowering or volatile emotional release. Generally speaking, it is rare that a blast of emotional energy actually elevates anyone—not the releaser, nor the one who is released upon, and certainly not an innocent bystander. In such cases, emotional energy is either splayed off in multiple nonfocused directions or inappropriately projected at another person. Either way, the benefit of the arising transformative potential is lost, since the person is unable to contain the energy.

Another popular strategy in handling emotions involves suppression. There are moments, of course, where some suppression is actually skillful. Should one become angry with another and the impulse to strike the other arises, suppression is clearly better than actually hitting the other person. However, when suppression becomes the strategy to prevent feelings from arising, it requires a strong act of will applied against the self. Practiced over time, suppression can even be sublimated, producing repression. Neither of these strategies are effective, either psychologically or spiritually, since such severe checking of the emotions does not address the issue of why they arose in the first place.

While these two strategies may look wildly different in their application, they hold something important in common. The habituated use of either is nothing but an attempt to manipulate or control the moment, effectively avoiding the direct experience of one's emotions. This movement "away from" separates one from the spiritual potential that may be present with the wave of emotional energy. Whether acting out or suppressing, both are avoidant strategies that dislodge one from the present moment.

What is needed is a third way to negotiate the emotional terrain— a way that allows one to be fully present for a charged emotional moment but without artificially superimposing either reactivity or suppression upon what is arising. Whether or not you have previously recognized it, it is possible to see every arising emotion as an open field of potentiality, particularly if the emotion can be greeted without the habituated movement of the mind. The emotional arising can become a creative possibility *if* and *when* one is able to experience the feeling content as a manifestation of one's enlightenment potential. Or we could even say that such is a manifestation that *expresses some quality* of one's already existing (even if not yet perceived) enlightenment.

The complicating factor in dealing with the emotional body is that often the emotional intensity that arises is accompanied by a dislike for the emotion. Thus, one must not only ascertain what to do with the energy of the particular emotion, but one must ascertain how to manage the emotional charge one carries *for* the emotion as well. Indeed, this complication can become multilayered very quickly

Put yourself in Arjuna's place for a moment. He was angry that he was being asked by Lord Krishna to undertake an activity to which he had a strong aversion. Likely, you can recall a time when you experienced anger when being asked to do something you did not want to do. Add to the anger the complication that in the moment you did not want to be angry and you found yourself dealing not only with the anger but also your own internal reaction (judgment) against being angry. Thus, you must find coping strategies to deal not only with the original anger but with your judgment of the anger as well. Perhaps there is the further complication of feeling some shame at being seen as an angry person by another, plus any judgment you might place on experiencing the shame.

With such rapidly compounding internal complications, if you are limited to choosing between reactivity and suppression, the loss of equanimity is understandable, even assured. In either case, you would simply be reacting to your own reactions, the net result of which is that projecting mind would be having a heyday! To complicate matters even further, perhaps you have begun to cut through the illusory veils of reactivity and suppression, and you find yourself nurturing dislike for both. Clearly, your chances of reclaiming equanimity become more and more remote.

To employ the third way postulated above, you would need to begin seeing the *energy* of anger—not the reactions *of* anger nor the reactions *to* anger—as a reflection of some portion of your enlightenment spectrum. If you can think of your enlightenment in terms of a spectrum of light (as, for example, a rainbow), such will work well for our purposes here. The rainbow of enlightenment contains within its wide spectrum a full range of radiant possibilities—from ultra-low frequency to ultra-high frequency. Within that spectrum of enlightenment, you not only find every emotional frequency, you find infinite energetic possibilities for its expression. If you can appreciate the energy of anger as a narrow bandwidth energy arising from the full spectrum, then there also arises a potentially instructive relationship with anger that cannot present itself if you are actively engaged in hating anger.

All emotional energies exist in a miniature spectrum within the great spectrum. For example, take the e-motion (or "energy in motion") you know as devotion. Pure devotion is a very spacious energy, and it exists at the high frequency end of a natural spectrum. At the low frequency end of the same spectrum is the constricted energy of addiction. The difference between what appears at the high end of the frequency range and the low end is radically different. (I use this example because the dichotomous ends are fairly easy to comprehend.) Whether or not you can see clearly the manifestations of high and low frequencies of all emotions is actually less important than understanding the principle here at work.

Clearly, the emotional energy of addiction is not a part of an enlightened person's frequency band because the enlightened individual identifies with the higher frequencies rather than the lower ones. Although the lower end of emotional frequencies may not be demonstrated in the brilliance of an enlightened person, still, the full spectrum of enlightenment contains the lower frequencies as well as the higher frequencies. The lower frequencies exist in alignment with all other possible radiant frequencies and are thus somewhere within the blend rather than singled out and focused for karmic projection.

The expression by which emotional energies are revealed results not from the pure frequency of a specific emotional energy but in a distortion of that energy. You could say those expressions are distortional reflections of the potential energies of enlightenment. Generally speaking, this distortional quality arises because at some level (personal or social) there is a negative judgment of the emotion. This judgment, layered on the original emotion, comes from the karmic movement of the mind. As a result, one may defend the emotional reaction, deny it or aggrandize it. In all cases, this layered-on energy distorts the original frequency of the pure emotion.

Clearly, these emotional complexes can be very complicated. In addition to the emotion itself, one's judgment of the emotion and one's reaction to the judgment, one must further negotiate a coping strategy for the judgment of the judgment—i.e., how one judges the defending, denying or aggrandizing tendencies. Although the route is circuitous, one is led right back to the options of reactivity or suppression.

Waking Up to Your Natural State

Is it any wonder that mastering the emotional body is seen as the last frontier from a spiritual perspective? The convolutions of mind are very complicated when it comes to emotions, particularly in societies where both individual egos and the collective ego are very big. Thus, to break free from the convoluted circuitry of ego mind, a different paradigm is imperative. It was, of course, to the old paradigm that the Buddha cried out his famous words, "Wake up!"

Waking up is precisely what is needed in the case of managing emotional intensity. Indeed, it is very much like you need to wake up from a dream to recognize and understand the dream. Perhaps you have a nightmare where some hideous monster is chasing you. Although the dream can be quite compelling, creating all manner of discomforting symptoms, when you awaken, you discover that there is no monster. In like manner, those intense, distorted or confused emotions are much like nightmares. When you awaken, you discover that they have no reality of their own.

Every emotion that arises presents some opportunity, even if obscure, to approach enlightenment. The mind's tendency to classify some emotions as "good" and others as "bad" stems directly from the karmic imprint that manifests in mental projections about the emotion. If one can move out of the "small picture" of judging the emotion and into the "big picture" of the enlightenment spectrum, then one can at least postulate that even the most negative and constricted emotional states have a vibrational relationship to the enlightened state.

Although hard for many to accept, the enlightened state is one's *natural* state. It is what exists beneath, before, behind and all around the artificial states of mind one experiences, for it gives rise to them from the infinite spectrum of enlightenment. The emotional states with which one often struggles arise to present an opportunity for seeing the full spectrum. When judgment of an emotion gets caught in the grip of projecting mind, one's focus is drawn off course. Instead of seeing the full spectrum, one sees only the projections *about* the emotion.

The Value of Direct Experience

Whether or not you perceive it, you are never separated from your enlightenment. It is without beginning, ever present and completely effulgent. The direct experience of any emotion provides a doorway to seeing the full spectrum of enlightenment. However, therein lies the problem. The very mind that ultimately perceives the full spectrum is the same mind that loses itself in various emotions and prevents you from discovering that full spectrum. In the first place, one must learn to directly experience emotional states without the karmic layering. Because the mind is so busy projecting *about* the emotional state, direct experience is usually precluded. Yet even if you could hold the projections at bay, another artifact of mind arises.

The moment you begin to probe an emotional experience, you release the experience. You trade *having* the experience for *investigating* the experience. The shift of focus causes you to lose the opportunity that was presented with the rise of the emotional state. Hence, the potential for a direct experience is lost.

Consider again the anger we treated above. As it arises, you feel its energetic presence in your body-mind. The moment you begin investigating the anger, however, something in your inner realm shifts and you lose the experience of the anger. In its place, you experience the investigation process, which tends to be reflective in nature. What might be felt as the aliveness of the experience is lost, since *reflecting on* the experience is quite different than *being in* the experience. In the former, perceiver and experience are separate. In the latter, delineation between experience and experiencer cannot be made. To reflect upon an experience, the mind must insert some kind of observational distance between the "who" (the one having the experience) and the "what" (the experience). In the separation, one trades "knowing" (the direct experience) for "knowing about." While "knowing about" is useful for many functional moments in life, it should never be confused with the direct experience of knowing.

The whole focus of education in the West is steeped in "knowing about," offering few opportunities for direct experience to students. Although in direct experience the sense of "I" is lost, in the indirect experience the "I" is always watching what it is doing, keeping track of what it is learning. If, for example, one must repeat a certain number of steps in a proscribed manner for a test, the "I" is probably evaluating its work as it learns the steps. In other words, the experiencing of a self is highly engaged. As an added consequence of the learning experience, the self is competitively graded against all the other students. The "I" is so highly engaged that it cannot lose itself in the experience.

Have you ever watched a child of four or five years of age experience snow for the first time? This child will show you a direct experience! She will roll in it, taste it, smell it, throw it in the air, possibly even put bare feet in it! The experience is direct and immediate, with no "I" doing, watching or evaluating anything. She will *know* snow—which is much different than *knowing about* snow.

In the Gnostic (i.e., knowing) experience, perceiver and perception are merged. Direct experience engages physical, emotional, mental and spiritual bodies—totally. For all its glory, direct experience can be threatening to the ego mind, which is continually looking for itself in the "having" of the experience. Direct experience lacks the observational distance needed for ego mind to find itself. To fall into a direct experience, the mind must release its hold on conventional reality— so laden with the personal reference points ego mind craves. If you consider the mystics of the great spiritual traditions, they all have the ability to lose themselves in the divine. To do so, of course, requires the dissolution of those personal reference points, for they obscure the very experience the divine one is seeking.

As with the child in the snow, what induces direct experience is full openness in/to the moment and a completely absorbed attention. To allow whatever arises to simply *be*, without the judgments or other manipulations of ego mind, is to find the vicinity of direct experience. In this open and attentive state, one can allow even emotional pain—grief, fear, hatred, greed, selfishness, envy and so on—to dissolve into the spacious radiance of direct experience. When the mind's eye is fixed on the full spectrum of enlightenment, it is very difficult to find the small bandwidth of, say, anger. The effulgent glow dissolves the very self that steps into it.

In the Bhagavad-Gita, Arjuna finds himself severely compromised by allowing the controlling nature of his emotions to rule him. While his emotional reaction appears to come from his situation (or his resistance to his situation), the truth is that he is reacting to his mental projection about the situation. He steps out of the field of direct experiencing and into the indirect experience of his own projections. Lord Krishna attempts to bring him nearer to a direct experience by reminding him that when he fights, he should fight for the sake of fighting—not for victory or enjoyment or even disdain. He admonishes Arjuna to let go of his personal preferences regarding the situation and to simply stay in the experience before him.

Lord Krishna understood the value of direct experience—experience unencumbered with the emotional and mental gyrations that so announce the presence of karma. When one can just experience with the mind empty and open, even a mundane experience can provide access to enlightenment. Lord Krishna's remarks to Arjuna about delusion are both classic and powerful: "When your intelligence has passed out of the dense forest of delusion, you shall become indifferent to all that has been heard and all that is to be heard. When your mind is no longer disturbed by the flowery language of the Vedas, and when it remains fixed in the trance of self-realization, then you will have attained the divine consciousness" (2.52–2.53).

Had Arjuna been able to see the energies of his emotional reactivity as holding a vibrational relationship to his self-realization, he could have discovered himself *in* the direct experience of self-realization. This is true of every arising thought, feeling or action. To be in the experience rather than observing oneself having an experience is the real thing. While judging mind might argue, the energy of an emotion is neither "good" nor "bad." It just is. In fact, the notions of "good" and "bad" are arbitrary reference points for the "I," having been designated by projecting mind.

Train your mind to be peaceful and spacious in all events. Train your concentration faculty so you can hold it steady—not giving way to projecting or judging mind. Then you too will be undisturbed by the distracted ego mind, and glimpses of your true nature will arise in consciousness. Bringing fully focused attentiveness to emotional energies as you experience them can open you to vast possibilities. Because Arjuna could not see through the antics of his projecting mind, he had to engage in warfare. How differently the story might have turned out had Arjuna been able to pierce the veil of illusion that hid the truth about his emotions!

Assembling the Puzzle

It is possible for humanity to make a significant collective breakthrough in consciousness, particularly at the dawn of a new century. Until fairly recently, there have been so many seemingly interesting domains to conquer, dominate, control and exploit on the planet, and the analytical mind has occupied most of the territory. Analytical mind works pretty well for strategies of conquest, but in bringing the full force of creative mind toward realizing enlightenment, such linear functioning leaves gaping holes in the grander excursions of mind. For one thing, analytical mind functions best when independently extended, which makes the notion of global community a bit of a mystery, at least to analytical mind.

If you consider carefully the fruits of analytical "conquesting" mind, you are likely to find yourself asking, "Is this all there is?" You discover that the Earth has been polluted and raped, the air is toxic and lacking in oxygen saturation, and the oceans are full of various kinds of death. This should be enough evidence to convince humanity that the old domination mindset needs serious revamping—perhaps a symbolic lobotomy!

Humans on Earth and the Domination Mindset

If you study the world of nature, you discover that domination is simply not natural. Humans have come to believe it natural, having "normalized" domination among their own kind and over other species. Yet in truth, no example can be found in either plant or animal kingdoms to substantiate the premise. Elephants do not try to dominate zebras. In spite of the fact that elephants have tremendous strength and body mass, they do not attempt domination over other animals. Although predators may feed on other species, they do not dominate those other species, nor grow them as livestock.

Simply stated, the levels of cruelty demonstrated by humans since the rise of the analytical (or ego) mind are categorically unknown among other species. This relational difference between how humans interact with their world versus how animals interact with their world is directly attributable to the egoic emotion of greed. Although an animal might appear greedy when the stomach is empty, it appears quite different when the stomach is full. Even in the case of food, it is unusual for a wild animal to take more than meets its momentary needs, or to hoard food, calling it "mine." When the stomach is full, they walk away from the leftovers, allowing other beings to have their meals as well. Such is the natural system, which manages to provide a balance that somehow eludes the cleverest among the dominators.

When a culture loses touch with the needs of the planet that houses it or forgets its duty to care for the planet upon which it dwells, often a natural disaster will arise in the collective experience so that attention may once again be focused on the relationship between planet and culture. A cataclysm—or some event regarded as a disaster—is one of the few mechanisms by which domination mentality can actually be overridden, since analytical mind may thus be needed for survival rather than domination. Catastrophes usually facilitate a reorganization of priorities and can bring people together who might otherwise demonstrate no pretense at connection.

The catastrophe—or more precisely, the *experience* of the catastrophe—draws people together, and they are able to experience connection. When life is good, on the other hand (i.e., pocketbooks are full, there's plenty of food in the refrigerator), a false notion or projection arises that one can exist separate or apart from the rest of the world. Such has become the "normal" way of seeing in the collective ego mind, and the presence of this collective attitude allows domination mentality to arise. When one feels superior to one's neighbor or sees through the lens of a "haves versus have-nots" mindset, the seeds of domination are sprouting. If this way of seeing is accepted by one generation after another, eventually a disconnected state of coexistence rules the land, replacing the setting of genuine community. Please note here that it is only through an exaggerated belief in disconnection that one individual seeks to hurt another, for the perceived "other" is having no shared energetic continuum with the self.

One of the problems with the projected false notion of utter independence is that it often leaves people with no sense of purpose, for there is no shared community into or by which life purpose can be demonstrated. Individuals who hold stark isolationist constructs often feel no sense of mission or reason for having taken birth. As one investigates more deeply, however, there will arise a more truthful understanding of the collective assignment. Since there are so many wonderful life forms existing on Earth, there must be something that connects them all, and it becomes obvious that this connection must hold a relational component to Earth as well. Clearly, the habituated projections of collective ego mind regarding the illusion of separation must be healed if Earth is to take healing from the wounds she has suffered at the hands of human history.

The Diamond Net of Indra

In the ancient Hindu tradition, there is a wonderful teaching that is perhaps instructive for the twenty-first century. The ancient story goes by the name "The Diamond Net of Indra" and has inspired countless students of mystery for literally thousands of years. In ancient times, when one wanted to speak of vastness too great to comprehend, the number ten thousand was used. Although the number ten thousand may not seem all that large today, there was a time when it seemed altogether too vast for comprehension. Today, one might say ten billion to produce the same effect in the minds of listeners.

The ten thousand (or ten billion) stars of the universe, so the story holds, are all joined together by a kind of web or net, composed of such a fine filament that it cannot be seen by human eyes. Even so, it is so delicate that if any one being on any one planet so much as moves or has a thought, the entire universe via the net is affected. The vibrations of that thought or action set the intricate filament to vibrating, and the vibrations, no matter how subtle, are carried to virtually every atom in the universe. This finely woven filament, however, is indestructible, and even though the net itself is imperceptible to the human eye, it sparkles like a diamond—thus it is called a diamond net. When any part of the net experiences the vibrations of domination, subjugation or separation, the whole net is forced to replicate the flow of that energy along its filaments. Such would apply to any energetic frequency—greed, hatred, impoverishment, intolerance and so on—vibrating along the matrix of the diamond net.

The Rise of Reductionism and the Scientific Method

Consider for a moment the effects of reductionist propositions vibrating along the diamond filaments. Newtonian physics—which is at least partially responsible for the exaggeration of analytical mind—tends to reduce everything down to its least common denominator. Although such is viable enough in some settings to launch a rocket from a planet and successfully land it on the planet's nearest orbiting moon, it cannot reveal any qualitative information as to living your life, experiencing personal growth nor witnessing spiritual transformation. The mentality of reductionism necessitates a very linear way of thinking and values analytical mental functions more than any other application of mind. In short, it supports the notion of "I" as the basic reality and keeps object and subject perpetually separate.

Initially, reductionism opened the door to scientific investigation, which titillated the minds that were curious to comprehend the workings of the universe. It supported the arising of a field you now know as physics and helped humanity establish reference points that were thought to explain the world. The view that all things within the material realm are unequivocally separate from all other things provided the basis for all the Western sciences and was not seen as fallible by the scientific elite until the early twentieth century, with the birth of quantum physics.

As the universe and all its pieces were viewed in terms of separateness, it seemed an obvious fact that humanity should be understood in a like manner. In learning to manipulate the various pieces of physical reality, a sense of power at the ability to do so became part of the understood nature of reality. Over time Western science, working within what were called "the laws of nature," became recognized for its ability to manipulate the elements of reality, even to the eventual feat of landing a rocket on the Moon. The science needed to accomplish such was quite reductionist in nature and required superb mathematical precision as to distance, force, trajectory and orbital fields of both Earth and the Moon. When seen as a set of independent problems to solve, such allowed the kind of knowledge that could eventually accomplish such a wonder.

This kind of accomplishment, of course, substantiated the growing belief in the intrinsic value of analytical mind, and the scientific method was incorporated at all levels of experiencing from education to the corporate business world. Analytical mind became valued above other functions of consciousness and ultimately came to be seen as the greatest contribution of the human realm. If we inquire as to the degree that collective ego mind has been influenced by pushing the scientific method into all areas of life, we are left with three propositions to consider.

The First Proposition:
Human Development Has Reached Its Pinnacle

This first is the notion that life on Earth in the twenty-first century is basically as good as it is going to get. Human development has reached its pinnacle, and whatever happens to humans collectively from here on will be little more than interesting permutations of what now exists. Physical reality is seen as the primary or basic reality, which is not necessarily drawn from any other reality. From this perspective, it is basically useless to worry about future generations inhabiting the planet, since the planet will soon be completely depleted and unable to support life.

The problem, of course, with this version of "reality" rests in the fact that because every part of life is viewed as an extension of the physical realm, vast and multidimensional levels are excluded. Likely, this proposition at least partially underlies the magnitude of depression that afflicts so many at the current time. It may also be a significant underpinning force to the emphasis modern materialism plays in the developed world today.

One of the excluded levels of consciousness thus far is what could be called *contemplative mind*, a state of consciousness that can readily move into mystery with faculties of perception unknown to analytical mind. Contemplative mind is not threatened in the absence of linear, logical answers to the big questions. In fact, it is neither influenced by nor impressed with the reductionist rationale analytical mind demands. Contemplative mind requires no analytical distance between perceiver and experience, and while offering something analytical mind would find principally intangible, the activities of contemplative mind both nurture and sustain the soul. Contemplative mind is the ground of being for the mystic, functioning in a manner more akin to a hologram than goal-directed linearity. Whereas analytical mind can describe experiences, contemplative mind responds to what we might term the "alive presence" within an experience. Contemplative mind both understands and relates to the presence of the numinous, responding to that which can neither be seen nor known by the physical senses and/or analytical mind.

If you were to read a treatise on the Moon, analytical mind would likely prefer the documentation of the scientist who has measured every nook and cranny of the Moon. Contemplative mind, however, would prefer the account of the poet-philosopher who speaks in terms of magic and mystery, perhaps exploring Moon as mistress. The scientific account may be interesting, but it cannot inspire a numinous state to arise within you, nor touch your soul, nor traverse the abyss, nor circumambulate the parameters of the inner universe. The scientist and poet tell different kinds of truth. The scientist describes, and the poet hints at relational possibilities that can expand consciousness and invite connection.

Because physical matter is the basis for being in a physical reality, it does deserve the attention of analytical mind with the implementation of the scientific method. But because the human being is really more than the sum of its parts, something more is needed for fuller comprehension. Consider the double-strand helix that supports your DNA—the basis for a living physical body. Whereas analytical mind concerns itself with the mere physical basis for being, contemplative mind inquires further. Studying the double-strand configuration, contemplative mind asks what such might mean at the level of cosmic expression. Rather than looking only at the genetic basis for a human being, contemplative mind inquires into the basis for *beingness* and postulates that the DNA strand is only a microcosmic representation of something much vaster. Contemplative mind can entertain the direct parallels between being and beingness, whereas analytical mind generally chooses not to wade in the depths of beingness.

Cracking the code for the human genome has become one of the great points of interest for the twenty-first century. Analytical mind will delight in all the raw data to be gleaned, perhaps for decades to come. Contemplative mind, however, will see the symbolic relevance of the double strand, holding that it must be predicated on some greater model of the same "truth" at a higher vibrational level. That higher frequency must therefore support beingness at all levels, not only for the human and animal species, but for every other phenomenon that can be observed and/or explored in this cosmic experience.

Hence, a correspondence can be made to the two fundamental parameters for beingness: time and space. These can be considered the spiritual genetic material for beingness in the cosmos, which correlates to the double-strand helix that supports the physical DNA spiral. Contemplative mind would argue that one of the DNA strands draws from the continuum known as space, the other from the continuum known as time.

Looking carefully at those two broad continua, contemplative mind can actually observe the basis for beingness. The strand (continuum) of space corresponds to matter, for matter takes up space. The strand (continuum) of time corresponds to consciousness. It takes both matter and consciousness to support beingness in the physical cosmos. Although all of the permutations on each cannot possibly be demonstrated by the example of a single planet or even a single solar system, one can at least look at the physical realm and make certain leaps into the para-physical realm. In so doing, one combines the strongest faculties of both analytical mind and contemplative mind.

The Three Rungs of the Space Continuum

What one finds on the space strand/continuum/ladder is a succession of rungs. The first corresponds to the mineral kingdom, the function of which is to generate a basis for stability of structure. Although you have learned from analytical mind that all matter may exist in one of three states (solid, liquid or gas), these three states are not readily observable in the mineral kingdom. Indeed, it takes tremendous energy in the form of heat and pressure to change the physical state of a rock. You primarily observe the mineral kingdom in the solid state, although you recognize that it exists in a liquid state at the Earth's core. The gaseous state, however, is something you must postulate, for while such is not observable on planet Earth, it is conceivable to most people that minerals could convert to a gaseous state *somewhere* in the universe where temperatures are sufficient to create such modifications. Although there is an encoding of stability within the minerals, such cannot literally be called consciousness, for it lacks the ability to interact with others of its own kind and affords little or no ability to shift on its own.

The second rung of the space continuum supports the plant kingdom, where a level of awareness can be observed that is not demonstrable in minerals. While plants do respond to their environment and do have the ability to mutate as a species, one cannot see that either process is conscious. In plants, the awareness is strictly tied to the morphology (the form and function) of the plant, and this is true even in terms of responsiveness to humans. Those plants that have had interactions with humans for generations—houseplants and domesticated garden plants—do, in fact, respond more readily to the bio-energy field of humans than do plants that have never been domesticated. This response has actually been measured by some and demonstrates the premise that plants can shift awareness levels. This awareness shift, however, is not self-generated, but comes about as a result of species modification due to exposure to the human field of radiant energies. Therefore, although plants are aware in some capacity, such cannot actually be termed conscious.

The third rung on our space continuum supports the animal kingdom. There is a marked difference in the complexity of awareness in animals from that of plants and minerals. The responsiveness to the environment is exquisitely heightened, as well as the responsiveness to minerals, plants, other animals and humans. The ability to communicate is obvious, as is emotional complexity. Interestingly enough, the more animals are around humans, the more they demonstrate the ability to self-generate awareness shifts toward the human level. Although animals are not self-aware in the way humans are—having the inner expression of a conscience, the ability to create complex personal agendas and strategize responses in multiple creative layers, and/or the ability to manipulate complex symbols—consciousness is clearly present.

Thus, it can be seen at the level of the third rung that, while matter can contain and utilize consciousness, consciousness is predominantly driven by the requirements of matter: food, shelter, comfort and relationship within their own family grouping. Although these basic needs are readily observable in animals of the wild, animals keeping human company reach out for social relationship with humans and with other animals not in their own family. Indeed, it is as if the definition of "family" broadens to include many species outside their own genetic line. In either case, however, the recognition for the value of or need for spiritual attainment is not present.

The Three Corresponding Rungs on the Time/Consciousness Continuum

As a matter of balance, one must postulate three corresponding rungs, or levels of awareness, on the time/consciousness continuum as well. The first or human rung/level is the first state in which consciousness defines matter. As was noted with the rungs of the space/matter continuum, just the opposite is true—matter defines the consciousness it contains. Clearly, the shift to the time/consciousness continuum demonstrates a huge shift in the reality that may be expressed. Although it is true that there are individuals in the human category who seem to demonstrate that their matter defines their consciousness, such is not actually true. Of course, on the first level/rung for the continuum of consciousness, there will be examples of those reflecting both the rungs on the space/matter continuum as well as higher rungs of the time/consciousness continuum. Clearly on this continuum, consciousness becomes increasingly complex, with wide variances expressed by way of the infinite potential relationships of matter and consciousness.

What must here be noted, however, is that the first rung, or human level, is a developmental level in which consciousness is still in training, so to speak. This is the level in which spiritual education takes place and provides the means whereby one may break out of the box of limitation. Indeed, this is the direction to which spiritual education points in every tradition, even if one tradition sees the goal of that education differently from another. One of the notable characteristics of human consciousness that differs from consciousness in the animal kingdom is the presence of self-doubt, peculiar to the human psyche but which is absent as succeeding higher rungs on the consciousness continuum are negotiated. Although it may be difficult for some ego minds to bear, it is both useful and instructive to consider the human state to be the beginning step for the embodiment of consciousness.

The next higher rung supports the consciousness level of what have been called ETs, or extraterrestrials. Due to much popularized science fiction, there are those who confuse ETs with what are called aliens, and although both exist, these two terms are emphatically *not* interchangeable. Although a lengthy description of aliens is certainly possible, suffice it here to say that they are holographic projections from some of the murkier collective experiencing of the past.

For example, assume for a moment that multiple generations have nurtured negative premonitions surrounding the meaning of the appearance of a comet in the night sky, generating terror at seeing a comet. Because the creative power of the mind is so astounding, a kind of archetype arises, imbued with what seems to be its own life from the projections of so many terrified people. The archetypal "entity" is said to be holographic because people of any time can step into it, thereby allowing their entire experience to be modified and perhaps dominated by it. As the terror projections regarding the comet and its perceived negative potential are vibrated out along the thin filament of light (remember our discussion of the diamond net), the archetype is held, you might say, within the net, available for conscious beings at many levels to experience. (You might like to speculate here about the differences possible for analytical mind and contemplative mind.)

In earlier times, people nourished fears of volcanoes and earthquakes, imbuing both with mystical powers over "mere" human beings. Fortunately, few hold such beliefs today but may have replaced such with beliefs in menacing evil beings from outer space, imbuing them with like powers. It is the collective belief in such things that creates these entities, but they are called alien because they stand outside the creational scheme for Earth. Simply stated, they are holographic projections of massive negative, often fearful thought. The power of group projection is very strong indeed and a viable creative force with which to be reckoned.

Thus, these collective projections take on the characteristics of a living entity as projected and can be accessed by anyone who harbors a fear of such or who, for whatever reason, has the karma to experience them. Some—particularly those of the archetype of the evil entity from outer space—have even been imbued with awareness. Such awareness does not come from the Source of All Being but rather from collective creative projection. Clearly, they are alien to the consciousness continuum.

ETs, however, are those beings who have evolved beyond the level of human consciousness but who choose physical embodiment as a means to help humans find the next step on the consciousness continuum. (It is important to avoid creating dogma here that will only later snare the analytical mind.) Standing between the human level and the level of the cosmic being, ETs move freely in and out of physical form. On planet Earth, the form taken is generally that of the recognized human form, or Adam Kadmon model. There are two reasons for this: The first is that the earthly human form is easy to manifest among humans, since the human consciousness all around holds the creative parameters for manifestation. Secondly, until humans evolve to a state where they can accept other physical forms as potentially higher consciousness forms, it is difficult to create the necessary relationship with humans to facilitate their growth. In other words, it is important for humans that they not designate ETs as "alien," since such would only reinforce the holographic projection that these aliens exist within the scope of creation and are seeking to compromise humanity.

Remember, the first rung on the consciousness continuum must be stabilized prior to the higher rungs manifesting, just as the mineral kingdom was stabilized before Earth could support a plant kingdom. Here the use of linear thought is helpful, since such is how analytical mind generally perceives time and experiencing. Although a case for nonlinear flow could certainly be made, it is likely that such would complicate the learning process for those who experience only linearly. For those who are able to comprehend creation evolving beyond the limits of time and space, know that while these examples cannot categorically be said to be "true," they can provide models for analytical mind to make the contemplative leap necessary for the growth in consciousness under consideration.

ETs, then, are likely the next type of consciousness to take embodiment at a physical, earthly level. Such has already happened in other star systems, and the presence of Indra's diamond net affords the possibility for Earth to follow suit. If ETs appeared in their natural bodies, very few people (if any) could see them. Although the level of consciousness they hold allows travel from star system to star system without spacecraft, the human form cannot afford the ease of such movement. Hence, the taking of human form is done solely for the purpose of aiding humans and not to benefit the ETs in any way. From a linear perspective, you could say you are living at a point in time when you are only just beginning to tap one end of the spectrum of consciousness available for physical embodiment. Indeed, contemplative mind can readily grasp that the human condition is simply not as developed as it will become and that the real basis for human beingness is not the material realm but the realm of consciousness.

The third rung/level on the time/consciousness continuum has yet to manifest. Indeed, most humans cannot as yet even imagine such a state, and because this level of consciousness has not previously taken physical form on planet Earth, there simply are no collective memory banks to access to aid humans in understanding just what this state of awareness might be like. Just as the animal kingdom demonstrates the presence of a significant development in consciousness beyond that of the plant and mineral kingdoms, so this third level/rung on the time/consciousness continuum will, at a much finer vibratory level, mirror that pattern. Of course, before such a level of consciousness manifests in physical embodiment, we must first discover what is possible in terms of evolutionary development for the other two levels.

In other words, the presence of ETs in physical embodiment, continuing their own evolutionary process, will change the potential for humans. As humans learn to ground greater possibilities for the race, that stronger foundation will allow for greater potentialities to arise in the spiritual development for ETs. As these two levels support each other in expansion and growth, a greater potential will result for that which is as yet "unmanifest" to bring into manifestation. It is quite likely that the physical form these greater beings take would not even be visible to the now-existing human race. As greater awareness becomes available to those in human form, however, finer and finer vibratory levels will be experienced and appreciated. Humans will eventually be able to see ETs, not only in their grossest form, but in their higher frequency forms as well. This change in human perceptive ability (which has been opening to greater and greater numbers of people during the past thirty years) is actually a signal that the first rung/level is beginning to draw significant energy and awareness from the higher potential second level.

The Second Proposition: Each Thing Is Separate

Returning to our consideration of the offerings of traditional science, the second proposition offered is the belief that each thing manifesting does so separate and apart from every other thing. Although analytical mind may hold to the notion that the self is separate from every other self, from nature and from the cosmos, contemplative mind simply knows otherwise. Without denying the appearance of separation, contemplative mind can realize that the notion of separation lies within the foundation of every kind of injustice that has arisen to afflict sentient beings the world over.

Whether creating wars, pillaging and raping communities as well as Earth, or speaking cruel words in a moment of negligence, all such behaviors arise from a belief in the notion that self is separate from all others. It is pointless indeed to deny the appearance of separation, but it is grossly confining to assume separation is the only explanation for what is. Whereas analytical mind may not understand a statement found in of one of Rumi's love poems, contemplative mind understands the intrinsic truth of his statement: "True lovers do not suddenly meet one day; they are in each other all along."

The ego mind looks at another and wails, "I cannot be him; he certainly cannot be me. We are so different!" While such is how it appears, one must remember that the maturation of consciousness is not quite finished at the human level, and one must allow the possibility that virtually all things are different in reality than the way they conventionally appear. Perhaps in considering a plant, the ego mind shrieks, "Just look at it; I'm not like that! I don't have those funny leaf things, and I'm not green! Surely we are not the same!" As you investigate more deeply, however, you come to discover that you *are* the same thing—both you and the plant are the manifestation of the life force within, and that life force is the same in both expressions. The forms are different, necessitating different functions. The "stuff" of life, however, is the same in both you and the plant.

You live in a time when analytical mind is exploring what has been termed the third era in medicine. The first era was based strictly on allopathic medicine, which relies almost entirely on drugs and medical interventions for explaining the healing process. The second era of medicine was also called mind/body medicine and hinged on the huge discovery that if one's attitude is firm, it is harder for the body to remain infirm. It also afforded experimentation with all manner of alternative methods for working with the body as a manifestation of the mind rather than something separate from the mind.

The third era of medicine holds that one's physical health or state can be affected by the thoughts, ideas and/or attitudes of others. In the third era, there has been "scientific" documentation—"proof" to analytical mind—that such things as prayer, meditation, healing circles and an open mind devoid of negative projection can positively affect one who is ill. Finally, what the third era affords is an approach to medicine or healing wherein applied science acknowledges a connection in consciousness that suggests humans are indeed *not* separate from one another.

Perhaps this third era will lead to a fourth era, wherein it is determined that consciousness is alive and can be understood as One. Perhaps it will be further determined that this One split itself into innumerable little pieces, imbuing each little piece with the potential to recognize itself when confronted by or with another little piece. Clearly, perceiving in terms such as these will undoubtedly stretch the confines of consciousness as experienced by the masses on the primary rung of the time/consciousness continuum.

The Third Proposition: Physical Reality Is All That Exists

The third proposition of conventional science holds that physical reality is all that exists, whether one speaks of the world or of the universe. If you cannot measure it, test it in the laboratory nor probe it with the five senses, it simply does not exist. With the rise of knowledge about quantum physics, however, this notion is beginning to feel the pressure of expanding minds, for quantum physics is the only branch of modern science that allows the state of "don't know" to be as creatively viable as known conditions and causes.

In the early 1980s, French scientists demonstrated that two subatomic particles that have been connected, even if subsequently separated by vast distances, somehow remain connected. If a change is precipitated in one, the other changes as well. Analytical mind has no explanation for activities such as these, because since all particles are separated (or at least appear to be), they should have no effect upon each other. Contemplative mind, however, places more meaning in connection than in separation, for it is able to grasp the difference in that which is and that which only appears to be. Indra, having thrown out his magic net, touches ten billion stars, uniting them with the fibers of light. Those fibers—so fine that they cannot be seen by the human eye, nor with any human aids to the eye—connect all celestial bodies of the universe in such a way that any happening on any body is immediately transmitted through the fine, living filament to all other bodies. In fact, in a single creative moment, an entire universe can be changed.

In truth, such is not so different from the intelligence contained in your body. Like the diamond web, fascia tissue literally touches every part of your internal body. It envelopes the muscles, surrounds the organs, lines the mesentery and weaves its way among all your tissues, functioning as the primary instrument of tissue communication. It knows your stress patterns as well as your organic weaknesses and strengths. Like your mind, your fascia constricts when influenced by karmic imprints, and it informs the entire body of such things as the fact that you may be carrying one shoulder a bit higher than the other or that you tilt your head off center a bit to the right. Those who work with bodies know it can sometimes take years to release holding patterns in a particular muscle, since it is not just the muscle that remembers but literally the entire body, as informed by the fascia. Although you may believe a specific pattern of contraction is in the shoulder, the fascia in the buttocks remembers and re-informs the body by sending the message back up to the shoulder.

Even within the realm of the purely physical, there are regions into which analytical mind cannot penetrate. For example, consider the miracle of gestation. A tiny ovum—no larger than the period at the end of this sentence—once fertilized, is encoded with all the information necessary to bring forth a human being imbued with the potentiality for great consciousness. How does that tiny cell know what to do? Even the most accomplished analytical mind cannot really explain the miracle or mystery of gestation. Analytical mind can count the cells or divide the term into gestation periods, but it cannot touch the magic of gestation, since magic communicates only with contemplative mind.

Gestation begins with a single cell, which starts dividing and replicating itself until it becomes a little piece of tissue. The tissue then begins to curve in on itself until it makes a sac, which will close into a pouch, which may then elongate into a tube. In fact, the entire human body is formed from a collection of sacs, pouches and tubes. One tube begets a brain stem; another stretches itself much longer and begets an intestinal tract. One pouch becomes the brain, which has a tube extending from it (the brain stem). That tube fills with a specific type of cellular material and begets a nervous system. That nervous system is exquisitely sensitive and replicates the diamond net of Indra, for that little gestating organ of cognition contains the light centers (or diamonds) that enfold this brain, encoding it with the potential for enlightenment.

There are many other mysteries that must be addressed—if indeed, they are addressed—by contemplative mind. For example, how is it that a rose plant will produce leaves that always look and function alike, even though the soil and climate conditions around the world may vary widely? From a reductionist point of view, when you isolate the biochemical agents in plant leaves that are responsible for engineering leaf form and function, you will discover that the ratio existing among those biochemical agents is very similar in rose leaves and in cauliflower leaves. However, these two leaves look nothing alike and function quite differently, emitting profoundly different fragrances. How is it that with what appears to be striking biochemical similarities, rose leaves always look like rose leaves and cauliflower leaves always look like cauliflower leaves? Most people simply do not approach such mysteries, for to do so is to step out of the realm of analytical mind and into the realm of contemplative mind.

When Contemplative Mind Awakens to the Miracle of Life

You may have noticed that as some people approach death, they have a profound awakening to life. Several years ago, a young man came to visit with me. He had AIDS and had begun the rude decline that comes at the end of the disease. Each day he could observe himself being more profoundly compromised than the previous day. The day he came to see me, he was held in a transcendent aura, completely at peace. From a deep sage awareness that was beyond his tender age, he remarked, "Life is such a mystery! How strange that in dying, I have learned how to live. Isn't it odd that I should have to die now?" His contemplative mind had been cracked wide open. In just walking down the block, he found himself in a mystical state wherein he literally *saw* the life force in the color green.

It was springtime, and in looking at the new buds and tiny leaves appearing on branches that lay bare all winter, he saw the life force. The color green appeared so vibrant that his senses could hardly tolerate the intensity. Of course, the nervous system is designed to be exquisitely sensitive so that everyone can take in the brilliant aliveness in all of nature. Most people, however, are so busy trying to escape their fears and bury themselves in their work, that seeing with the openness of contemplative eyes has fallen away from the "normal" experience. Yet in the face of death, often those eyes are reopened and the incredible mystery of life becomes perceivable. When contemplative eyes are wide open, there is no analysis of what is perceived—there is only the rich aliveness of the experience of perceiving that validates connection to the infinite in very mundane moments.

If you talk with veterans of war who were in situations where they were quite sure they would be killed within the day, they may tell you amazing stories. Some will admit that they felt most alive when death appeared certain. The colors in nature may have become so vivid in their moment-to-moment experiences that their senses could hardly bear the intensity. In this state of heightened awareness, the colors are not just pretty—they come to life, creating a vibrant dance. Although most do not perceive it, there is motion to color; it is not static. Until a person awakens to radical aliveness, however, that motion cannot be perceived by the senses. There is a saying that 99 percent of the world's population is asleep. The 1 percent who are awake, however, live in a constant state of amazement, for contemplative mind has opened and the miracle of life is palpable.

There is a great story that originated in Japan that demonstrates the power of focused contemplative mind. A Buddhist nun was out walking alone in the mountains. Enjoying the beauty of the scenery surrounding her, she wandered into an area where people did not usually walk, since there were many wild animals in the vicinity. She was startled from her ebullient trance by a sound on the path before her. As she quickly brought her full attention into the conditions surrounding her, she saw before her two tigers. In fright, she turned and ran. She ran for her very life and, glancing over her shoulder, noted that the tigers were gaining on her. Heart pounding, she suddenly found herself on a precipice. In her panic, she noticed there was a little vine growing from the rocks, hanging down the precipice. It appeared to be well anchored, so she grabbed hold of it and jumped over the edge.

Making a careful descent, she peered beneath her to see how far the drop to lower ground was. Although the vine would allow her to go near enough to the ground that she could simply release the vine and fall, she noticed that waiting at the base of the rock wall were two more tigers. To make matters worse, she drew her attention upward to where the vine emerged from the rock wall, and there above her were two rats gnawing on the vine. Understanding her fate instantly, she looked to one side. There, growing in the face of the rock cliff, was a beautiful strawberry plant with one perfect strawberry hanging in the sunshine. She reached out, just minutes from death, plucked the strawberry, placed it in her mouth and savored the taste of the most wonderful strawberry in her short life.

Analytical mind would not enjoy that strawberry! Contemplative mind, however, could be fully alive for the experience of the strawberry—even in light of the fact that the tigers below were about to have the nun as their dinner. We can be quite sure that the strawberry afforded her an experience of cosmic unity. Minutes from death, contemplative mind opened and she took on a radical aliveness, becoming radically present for a total and direct experience!

Analytical mind is rarely open to direct experience. Analytical mind requires the experience of distance between the observer and what is being observed. Since analytical mind cannot surrender to the aliveness of an experience (or analysis would be lost), it can never merge with the experience. Contemplative mind, on the other hand, does not perceive itself separate from the experience it is having, but it cannot arise until analytical mind surrenders its hold on both the experience and the "I" who is having the experience.

Another example of contemplative mind can be recognized in the recounting of a Westerner's visit to a monastery where there lived a renowned Zen archer. The Westerner was trying to understand "Zen mind," and since the mind state cannot be defined exactly, the archer provided a demonstration for the Westerner. Picking up his Zen bow, his arrows and a blindfold, the master counted sixty paces from the target and took his position there. As you may know, the Zen bow is not like a Western bow. It is very difficult to draw the string of a Zen bow, and untrained individuals cannot do it, no matter how great their physical strength. To make his point, the master blindfolded himself and held the bow in such a way that made it even more difficult to draw. Thus compromised, the master raised the bow and let an arrow fly, hitting his target right in the very center of the bull's-eye. To demonstrate that the first shot was no fluke, the master then positioned another arrow, and in letting the second arrow fly, he sliced the first arrow with the second, still wearing the blindfold!

In the West, shooting a bow is a highly analytical task. One must brace his or her stance for the weight and full force of the bow, take aim, estimate the distance to the target, apply the appropriate tension to the string, hold a concentrated focus on the target, and release the string with proper technique. To the Zen master, however, the exercise was all about the breath. With contemplative mind, the master can breathe in the universe and become one with it and all the forces it contains. With concentrated focus, his mind can merge with the bow, with the arrow and with the target. To accomplish the goal, he must accomplish the complete release of the analytical mind so that the contemplative state of Oneness with the universe may be available to him. In that moment, is there a difference between master and bow? The answer, of course, is outside the reach of analytical mind.

Moving Beyond the Tenets of Conventional Science

The diamond net of Indra supports and contains the knowing that allows mastery of such accomplished feats. From the perspective of such mastery, one can clearly see beyond the tenets of conventional science here treated—that human development has reached its pinnacle, that each thing can be independently identified and is separate from all other such things, and that only those pieces and systems that can be perceived by the physical senses can be called "real." Viewed from the perspective of the Zen master, however, the cumbersome manipulations and distancing tactics of analytical mind offer little more than stumbling blocks to the direct experience of being. The diamond net, you see, communicates only with contemplative mind.

Perhaps if your contemplative mind is now engaged, it may occur to you that you are in fact the vehicle through which those ten billion stars shine. The delicate, sensitive diamond web is a web of consciousness, which simultaneously supports creation and operates upon and through creation—not only as you see it, but also in all the infinite variations it has the potential to be. Contemplative mind transcends the boundaries of analytical mind and is the vehicle by which karma is transcended, the mind is liberated and all notions of duality are dissolved.

10

Death and the Mind

D eath is the ultimate "mind trip." Parts of the journey can only be described as hallucinogenic, although no reliance on chemical or biological substance is needed to provoke this incredible "mind-altering" experience. The way the mind functions in life sets the precedence for how it will function in death—at least in the initial part of the journey. The actual experience is determined in large part by the guidance—or lack thereof—provided by the conditions to which one has been acculturated, as well as the karmic predisposition to watching the mind unravel and dissolve.

The act of awareness separating itself from the physical body proves beyond question that the designated self is not the body. In life individuals may struggle with understanding just what the self is, often contemplating that although it is *not* the body, it must reside somewhere *in* the body. Many allege that the self must reside somewhere in the brain. However, in millennia of surgical procedures having been contrived upon the brain (even as far back as ancient Egypt), no surgeon has ever found the self, nor any neural demarcation in the tissue that might indicate the presence of a self. In fact, the act of dying proves that the notion of a self is not a part of neural processing, for the brain dies and rots. Even so, awareness is not impeded by brain death, nor is this notion of self.

Experiencing the Death Process

It is perhaps useful to examine the process of dying at this point—less from the physical perspective, however, and more from the perspective of the awareness. Indeed, much can be learned about living in coming to understand the transition of dying. Of course, other than from a physical perspective, what is often regarded as dying is not what is actually going on. It is appropriate and necessary to drop the cells from time to time, for the issues one seeks to clarify in a given life are in fact encoded in the cellular material. As the popular slogan put forth by body workers in the 1980s goes, "The issues are in the tissues!" Thus, one of the purposes for death is to free the awareness from the cellular encoding that one took in a given life. Every time the awareness releases a specific configuration of cells, proof is rendered to the awareness—which congealed for the experience—that the "I" is indeed *not* that cellular material, no matter how strongly identified that "I" might have been with the past cellular package.

In like manner, this "I," while not the body, can neither be the mind. Indeed, for most people, the sense of being an "I" is strongly grounded in the experience of mind, for it is the mind that recognizes the "I" and uses the "I" to project the *bakchaks* from other life experiences. Although there is unquestionably a functional relationship between the "I" and the mind, they are not the same thing. Ultimately, all will discover that there is, in fact, no "I," even though awareness continues lifetime to lifetime and throughout the interesting spaces in between.

As one nears the point of death, radical changes take place in the mind. In the first place, the five senses begin shutting down, which radically shifts one's ability to connect and communicate with others around him or her who are not dying. As the physical senses begin to close off, the dying person becomes less responsive to stimulation through touch, taste, smell, sight and hearing. Of course, person to person, this process amends itself depending on several factors: the person dying, the disease or physical complication that is facilitating the death process, the lessons that are arising in the moment, and the ability to grasp the spiritual dimension that is dawning.

All of these factors will be somewhat complicated by the karmic factors in place from past death experiences, the cultural conceptions regarding dying and the greater or lesser ability to apply any new and/or useful skills gleaned in the life that is coming to a close. As the organs also shut down, the metabolic, circulatory and respiratory processes undergo radical changes as well in order to facilitate the release of awareness that governed each and every cell in the body. In some cases, the actual point of transition comes quickly. In other situations, an individual can remain on the precipice of death for days. This is so because of the factors and influences mentioned above, as well as the relative degree to which a given package of cells are able to release the awareness they hold. As in every other matter in life, the differences demonstrated from person to person can be quite wide ranging.

As the awareness parts company with cellular material, the separation is radically noticeable at the physical level but less observable from the perspective of the awareness. In fact, because the "I" has been accustomed to referencing itself by its own physical mass, it continues to do so even though technically the two are no longer symbiotically joined. In the initial phase, the awareness is drawn to a vibrant white light, which is so compelling as to block out awareness of any and all other stimuli. Initially, the awareness of the bright light is actually stimulated by the absence of oxygen to the optic nerves, embedded deep within the brain. This is a wonderful service of a dying brain, for it physiologically mimics the soul's journey into light in such an intense way that the dying individual cannot help but pay attention.

The Transition through the Tunnel

What follows has often been described by those who have had near-death experiences as a rapid transit through a brilliant tunnel of light. The light is so compelling that the individual has no awareness of anything but the searing quality of the light and the sense of rapid movement. Most perceive they are being hurled through space—granted, very bright space—at an uncontrollable rate of speed. What is actually happening is that the awareness is rapidly expanding, for it is no longer contained in a finite package defined by time and space.

Just as the dying process varies from person to person, so does the level of expansion. Although everyone has the sense of moving very fast and covering a great amount of perceived distance, the actual degree of expansion is dependent upon one's spiritual attainment. Clearly, one who has accomplished great expansiveness in life is capable of greater expansion after life. However, the greater the prison of suffering that confined one in life, the less the capacity for expansion into light after death.

What is actually happening is that awareness, unbounded by physical tissues, is trying to expand to encompass the cosmos. If one is capable of undergoing this shift in consciousness purely from contemplative mind, the experience would be direct and immediate, and likely one would have some understanding of exactly what is happening. This experience is somewhat similar to clasping one's fist very tightly and then suddenly opening the hand to its most extended position. In one moment, the hand is tight and contracted, and in the next it is stretched open to its widest capacity. However, since most individuals live their lives in the analytical mind mode (which functions linearly), the perception of the experience follows suit—that is, it *appears* to the mind that one is being dragged or hurled through a great expanse at an incomprehensible velocity.

Of course, if the one who is dying has no understanding of the process, that lack of knowledge also informs the process. Rather than feeling at peace with the process and cogently curious, one might find the tunnel experience terrifying. In this case, the tunnel journey seems to create an out-of-control state that exacerbates existing fears, whatever their type. Just as in life, success in death requires surrender to the process and forces that are operating in the moment. For those who fear and fight the process, however, even the journey into light can be perceived as a torturous event.

What has also been happening in the transition through the tunnel is the opening of the psychic centers. In the dying process—particularly for those who die in a comatose or hypo-lucid state—the psychic centers have been gradually opening as the gates of awareness (the five senses) have been closing. In individuals who die suddenly, however, the psychic centers open in the perceived journey through the tunnel of light. By the time the rapid transit appears to have stopped, the psychic centers are generally open and are functioning much like the five physical senses previously functioned. This allows for perception to continue, even though there are no bodily sense organs operating through which perception can occur. Thus, the notion of the "I" is still alive and well, so to speak, and one is able to observe and participate in the experiences that continue to arise.

As the perception of soaring through the tunnel of light comes to a close, most perceive themselves as still in their familiar body, often looking down at their own body and even seeing themselves dressed in certain items of clothing. Of course, what is actually happening is that the mind is projecting a familiar image of the "I," which it believes and attempts to reinforce. At this point, usually the awareness begins to look around and describe to the mind what is going on. This is often the great state of peace and calm knowing about which those who have had near-death experiences speak after their awareness returns to their physical bodies.

Generally, one finds oneself suspended in an unimaginable and oceanic continuum of grace and pure love. It is in this state of suspended animation that one remembers why she took birth. Often, one will become aware of all the opportunities of love that surrounded her in life—even if she was unable to see them while in the moment of their arising. More profoundly, one remembers that she came from this oceanic love and likely took birth to remind others of the infinite force of love from which all sprang and to which all return again and again.

Undergoing the Life Review Process

It is from this experience of being suspended within unimaginable love and grace that most do what has been called the life review. For many, of course, this process actually starts prior to dying, and if one is fortunate enough to have the time and clarity to begin the review process before separating from the body, it is very helpful to the process that comes after death. It is indeed a provocative moment to experience oneself suspended in the very love that supports the cosmos. If one can open to the powerful force of all that love operating upon the "I," one can open to enlightenment as well. You could say that this is the first opportunity to become enlightened after leaving the physical body. Although there will be other opportunities afforded as well, this is perhaps the sweetest.

Of course, if one has the karma to recoil from love rather than opening to it, then one would not likely be able to review his own life from the stance of compassion. Rather, that one might feel the effects of all his non-loving moments in the life just vacated. He would undoubt-edly feel the pain of those moments, but rather than hold all in com-passionate neutrality, he might project the experience to be some cruel awareness separate from the "I" as sitting in judgment of him. In other words, although pain may be experienced from this incredible place of love, it is felt in a context that neither invites compassionate review nor engenders compassion for the return flight. Clearly, in this event, this one would not likely be able to open to enlightenment, even though surrounded by and/or suspended in enlightenment. Thus, the greater one's capacity to open to love in life, the greater one's potential for dis-solving into love at this important stage of the journey.

It is in this beautiful state of suspension in divine light and love that one often meets her spiritual teacher, guides, angelic beings and a host of others willing to reflect the infinite love of creation to her as she makes the transition. Again, this part of the experience is directly proportional to one's ability to open to the Infinite. If the encounter thus far is to be an NDE (near-death experience), this is the point at which she will be "called back" to the physical realm.

Many will experience a special teaching or blessing and then be instructed to return to the physical body they left. Others will feel that they were granted an opportunity to peer into "heaven" but will recognize that there is so much more they are capable of continuing back in physical reality. Either way, getting back into a body can be an interesting experience—particularly if the body is encoded with phys-ical pain and/or impairment. In such situations, the one who comes back does so from a perspective of kindness and generosity toward those they may be capable of aiding.

The Stupor Phase

To those for whom the experience is not an NDE but the real thing, after the life review is complete, there will follow a stupor state in which the mind begins the unraveling process. During this time—which is often about the space of four Earth days—the mind literally splits in two. It is often during this stage that one begins to realize that he or she has died, which can be quite shocking if not realized prior to this point. For many, there is a feeling of being caught between the realms. Although they may actually desire to return to their loved ones, as well as to the myriad of things left undone, they recognize they cannot do so. Some individuals may actually feel they are being torn apart, with part of the mind adhering to the past, usually wishing/trying to change the past, and part of the mind attaching to the future, desiring to move from this state of paralysis. If the experience of paralysis is great enough, it will likely be followed by a sense of losing consciousness—much like fainting is experienced in physical form. Such provides a loss of contact with both the past and the present.

Should things run amok in this phase of the journey and one become obsessed with the physical plane—perhaps even denying his own death—he might find himself entering the condition know as an earthbound spirit. In this condition, he actually experiences himself almost identically to the way he experienced himself when in physical form. That is, he will continue to project the image of the "I" in a familiar way, complete with remembered clothing and all manner of conventional familiarities. The intense focus on the physical realm and the effort to resurrect himself in the familiar physical form gives rise to a state of entrapment. Little by little, he will recognize he has died, but the intense focus on trying to re-create himself as physically alive prevents him from going on with the journey. Often, individuals in this state require a medium or one skilled in such areas to release them from their trapped condition.

Of course, it must be said here that this trapped state is a state projected by the mind. Although it cannot be said to literally be "real," clearly it is really experienced. While some traditions would classify this condition as one of the regions of hell, it is important to recognize that the state has been created by the mind's projections. Just because one dies in a physical sense, that physical death does not limit the mind's ability to project, for some have spent hundreds of Earth years as an earthbound spirit.

Since the projection comes from mind (based on its prior physical experiencing), release from this state or condition requires the services of one who is still in physical form to facilitate the type of liberation. In truth, some in this state are able to recognize the projection of the earthbound condition and simply release it from their fields of awareness. In such cases, that one would have the experience of being dramatically "liberated" in the moment of awakening to the projected field.

It is important to understand that any time in life or death the mind can release a projection, freedom is available. That being said, the perception of what freedom should look like is for the most part also a projection. Situations like the one mentioned above (the earth-bound spirit releasing its projected condition) make clear the necessity for having a method of working with the mind. Challenging the mental projection is a skill of profound magnitude in both life and in death. One need not wait until finding himself or herself in an earth-bound state to dismantle the karmic projections. Indeed, the methods that work in life can and likely will serve in death as well. Just as what one learns about death can serve one in life, so what one learns in life can be very useful in death. In this case—dismantling the pro-jection—the process is twofold: learning the method and remember-ing to apply it.

The Journey of the *Bardo*

Upon the close of the stupor phase, one has the sense of sud-denly being awakened. The exact experience of this awakening varies widely, depending on the spiritual development of the indi-vidual consciousness. For some it may appear to be the gentle voice of the beloved teacher calling to awaken the aspirant. On the other end of the spectrum, one might experience the awakening as in awakening from a horrifying nightmare. In this latter case, he arises in fear, sensing that the nightmare is still continuing even though he feels awake.

While these two examples represent the ends of the experiential spectrum, every imaginable condition of awakening that falls between is open to experience as well. As this awakening happens, the mind reflects back to the state it experienced at the point of death, where the karma was being set for the lifetime to follow. This mind state is re-created, and the journey of the *bardo* begins. The word *"bardo"* simply refers to an in-between state. In this case, the term applies to the "time," or experiential flow, between lives. Just as life may be experienced as a journey, so the *bardo* also takes the form of a journey. It is a journey into the profound creative recesses of the mind—although to most, it may not appear as such.

One interesting aspect about this particular journey is that there are no diversions along the way; there is only the "I" and the mind, which becomes the field of experiencing. The different spiritual traditions that teach about this in-between experiential space do so using terminology relevant to the specific tradition. Suffice it to say, however, the journey is fueled by raw creative energy, which operates upon the points of nonclarity that still remain in the belief structure. Much like the experiences reported in the ancient Egyptian initiations, the mind is cracked open, and whatever beliefs and fears remain unaligned with truth are manifested by the intense creative forces at play.

As the many experiences arise in this journey, they will *appear* to be coming from something outside the parameters of the mind. For example, one might see her teacher beckoning from a distance. Seeing the familiar and kind face, she might begin to move toward her teacher. However, if she was afflicted in life with a doubting mind, the apparition may change suddenly, seeming to present her with a thousand beings who look like her teacher—still beckoning, but perhaps appearing to laugh with the shift in apparition.

In this type of experience, it is the reactivation of doubting mind that causes the apparition to change, and if she is able to recognize the projecting mind at work, the apparition will likely change again. This succeeding change, however, will not be based in doubting mind, nor will it stimulate doubting mind. However, should she identify with doubting mind (perhaps as in life), the apparition is likely to become more confusing and more doubt-producing. She might attempt going to the teacher, only to suddenly find herself in a strange maze with all the paths leading to dead ends.

If fear is also present, instead of dead ends, the maze may present paths that end in dangerous or profoundly frightening outcomes. Again, if she is able to recognize the apparent maze as a mental projection, it disappears. Moment to moment, she will be greeted with opportunities to see projecting mind without the diversions of life— such as the telephone ringing or some other event arising to pull your focus from the process at hand.

The directness and rapidity of projecting mind without diversion can, of course, be quite intense. Frequently, the one negotiating the *bardo* journey does not see through the mind's activity, believing whatever appears to be real. At times, his fears may take the form of monsters or demons. Once again, if these apparent beings can be seen as extensions of his mind—originating from the "I" and there-fore a part of the "I"—then both the apparitions and the "I" begin to dissolve. However, in the event he believes in the apparition, the "I" becomes more firmly fixed, perhaps seeing itself in opposition to the characters of the apparition and fleeing from them or fighting with them. In this case, the notion of duality is emphasized, which will only create more apparitions with symbolic characters arising to invite insight and awakening.

In a different kind of experience, one might hear her teacher's voice calling her name. Perhaps she turns in the apparent direction of the voice, but instead of seeing her teacher, she may experience an intensely bright light—so bright, in fact, as to have the feel of a laser beam or even a knife blade cutting into flesh. This light may be sur-rounded by lesser lights of soft colors that also seem to beckoning to her. How the mind projects meaning on to the experience of the lights will determine in large part how she is likely to negotiate the mind's terrain. If the laser beam feels as if it is cutting through flesh—even though the connection to flesh has been dropped—she might project that the laser light is dangerous and try to flee from it. On the other hand, if the mind projects a scenario in which behind the laser beam is actually the teacher, then she will move toward the light, will-ing to endure the pain but likely recognizing it too as a projection. In this case, the laser light, the pain and the "I" begin to dissolve.

Perhaps in yet another experience, the mind projects a salivating monster, which seems to be chasing the self, and an angel. If he believes the projection, he might attempt running to the angel for protection from the monster. However, such a belief is ill placed, for as he approaches the angel in desperation and fear, the angel dis-solves. On the other hand, if he can recognize that both images are mental projections, he is more likely to turn toward the salivating monster and greet it in love and compassion. To do such would dis-solve the projection.

Know that whatever one fears in life will greet her in death. In like manner, whatever one hates in life, she will sooner or later become. A common *bardo* experience is that of seeing oneself become a monster. Whatever one hated in life is symbolically re-created in the *bardo* as a monster. Having hated, she may be forced to see herself become the object of that hatred, or she might simply see herself becoming the hated monster. For example, if she hates snakes in life, she might have an experience in the *bardo* of not only becoming a viper but of becoming one that hideously destroys and eats Buddhas, or angels, or children. Again, if she can see that what arises in the experience is but an apparition of mind projected into the experience at hand, all the images will dissolve, thus creating an opening for healing—possibly even enlightenment.

Preparing for the *Bardo* Journey

In the traditions that teach aspirants how to negotiate the *bardo*, most teach that it need not be a frightening experience. In the *bardo*, just as in life, the most significant part of transcendence is simply to watch rather than follow the mind. The training given to negotiate the *bardo* well is identical to the training given to negotiate life well. In truth, the *bardo* experience is related to and reflective of the life experience. The main difference is that the *bardo* journey is compressed and lacks the diversions so prevalent in life, which divert attention from the mind and its activities.

In life, most fall prey to the illusion that if one does not master a particular level of consciousness at a given turn, there will always be another turn to do so just up ahead. Believing this illusion, some become lazy in doing their spiritual work, feeling that there will always be time later to do the work. Because of the intense nature of *bardo* experiences, however, putting off one's transcendent work simply is not an option. In life, as in the *bardo*, suffering comes from projecting mind. In life, however, this investigation of mind and the dismantling of projections is easily diverted, resulting in procrastination toward the very work that allows suffering to cease. In this case, one must again face the projections as they arise in the *bardo*. There is good news here, however, since one applies the same antidotes to suffering in the *bardo* that one would have used in life. Because the training for negotiating both life and the *bardo* is consistent, the antidote for suffering must also be consistent.

In certain Eastern cultures wherein the aspirant trains in life for a successful journey in death, meditation training is recognized to teach the skills necessary to interrupt the projection activity of the mind. Indeed, if meditation is efficacious in life, how can it be otherwise in death? Thus, spiritual students are trained to observe the mind. When a thought or apparition arises, he learns to simply drop the thought and return to a still placement of mind. The placement can be on silence, or on an image (*yantra*), or even on a set of words (*mantra*). Indeed, the meditator can place his full attention on an internal image of the teacher's face. As long as he holds to the image with full concentration, his mind simply cannot project. The student is taught to return his concentration to the object or image that is used in meditation when chaotic or confusing thoughts arise. Following this, instruction is given to remember the basics: (1) when the mind projects, there is suffering; (2) suffering arises in both life and death because one is attached to outcomes, either through desire or aversion; (3) since suffering has been completely transcended by the great spiritual masters of all times and all traditions, cessation of suffering is clearly possible; and (4) the way to stop suffering is through training the mind.

It is important to remember that the journey through the *bardo* is an opportunity to transcend all the levels of projecting mind that may have been missed or avoided in life. As the projections are dismantled, the mind dissolves into a profounder awareness. Of course, this is precisely what one tries to accomplish in life, for the mind's projecting activities actually obscure access to profound awareness. Mind is like a tangled ball of yarn, where the strands of clear awareness are caught in the projections of lifetimes. Of course, mind attempts to imitate this clear awareness, but it is limited in both function and scope by the projections it supports.

To use another metaphor, the mind can be likened to clouds. Consciousness, however—one's true nature in life and in death—is vast and open like the sky. Suffering arises whenever one identifies with the clouds (or projections), for her true nature does not shift with the winds of change. When her identity is so remarkably misplaced, suffering simply cannot be avoided. As she learns to use mental projections in a skillful way, however, the payoff extends beyond life—even beyond death.

As should be obvious by now in this text, if the mind is active, it is projecting. Learning to release the projections that do not serve to bring about enlightenment is clearly a skill of a well-trained mind. Yet there is another skill along these same lines that takes one to the next step, and that is learning to use projecting mind to take him ever nearer the goal. By way of a life example, suppose for a moment that he projects that another person is angry with him. From this projection, his mind takes off on its own journey, perhaps addition-ally projecting that the other is wrong and that the perceived anger is unjustified. Next his mind projects all the wonderful things the "I" has done for this other over the years and begins to feel critical of the other. From this point, his mind goes on and on, projecting, project-ing and projecting. Clearly, these projections make no contribution to either the enlightenment of himself (the projector of record) or the other person. The truth is, he suffers under the weight of his own projections, and it is likely that they will trigger suffering for the one who receives them as well.

One way to stop the suffering is to recognize projections as they arise in thought, then simply drop or release the thought or image just as one would do in the practice of meditation. Imagine you are sitting in meditation and a thought arises. In that moment you have a choice to make: either go with the flow of the thought and perhaps create a protracted fantasy, or simply notice the arising thought and drop it, returning to quiet mind. In like manner, when a projection arises, you can either go with the flow of the projection, creating protracted fantasies, or you can choose to simply drop it in the moment of its arising. Clearly, this latter practice trains the mind until it becomes facile with the practice, which will ultimately free the mind from its projections of, fantasies on and preoccupations with suffering. Going with the thought flow, however, can only per-petuate suffering. This practice of dropping the projection is a sig-nificant skill to master in life, since it works as well in the *bardo* for eliminating suffering as it does in the course of life. Although alone it may not open one to the full experience of enlightenment, it does at least get one out of the zone of suffering.

One can go even further with this practice, replacing the mind's original projection with the projection that a Buddha might have. For example, after noticing that the mind has presented the projec-tion that another is angry and after then dropping the projection, one might then project, "How profound is the light of awareness in this one!" Or, "Can I see the Buddha within this other part of myself?" Replacing ego projections with enlightened projections is beneficial for both oneself and the recipient of the projection as well. This practice is remarkably helpful as one prepares for his *bardo* journey. Just imagine what might happen if, when the monster apparitions arise, he could see each as an emanation of a Buddha!

Of course, one cannot experience enlightenment until she is able to *project* enlightenment. Further, if she can project enlightenment from the *bardo*, the projection is as empowered by the creative forces at work in the *bardo* as are, say, the projections of fear. These creative forces, if powerful enough to cause her fears and doubts to manifest with profound reality and ferocity, can surely produce no less of an effect on her projections of enlightenment! When she realizes enlightenment in the *bardo*, the whole experience of the *bardo* dissolves into a direct experience of the pure realm, sometimes also called *nirvana*.

For those who do not realize enlightenment in the *bardo*—indeed most do not—the journey from projection to projection continues, often with projections arising and manifesting so quickly that they seem to overlap each other. One is presented with a rush of continual material as his mind unwinds, offering up all its projections for manifestation. This process does empty the mind of its content, which should facilitate complete dissolution of the "I" through the continually changing images and experiences.

All too often, however, the *bardo* journeyer clings to the "I" in an attempt to establish some point of reference for the rapid assault on the mind. He may forget to apply the methods that can allow the mind to become completely transparent and dissolve. Usually this "I"-clinging arises from one form of fear or another. Some fears may have been carried from the previous death, others perhaps arose in his life just completed, and still others come from a lack of knowledge and/or understanding about the process he is undergoing. In all cases, however, his fear was allowed to take charge because his mind believed what it projected.

The Awareness Is Released for Rebirth

As mentioned above, as the mind is emptied of projections and "I"-ness, a veil ultimately descends over consciousness as the *bardo* journey comes to an end. The whole process takes approximately fifty Earth days, although the experience may seem much longer. At that time, the awareness is released for rebirth. Just as in life, it is possible to take a wrong turn in the *bardo*, which can complicate the journey or even extend it beyond the normal fifty Earth days. However, in most instances the journey is completed in that time. For most, the opportunities for enlightenment in the *bardo* pass unrecognized, and the cyclic pattern of existence simply continues. As mentioned above, the forces of karma drive most to seek immediate rebirth. For those spiritually awake enough to accomplish such, there is opportunity for integrating the *bardo* journey during the completion of the gestation period that follows on the physical level to prepare the next body.

Toward the end of the journey, there is a phase where the awareness—which at this point cannot exactly be called an "I"—is encouraged to invoke an appropriate birth. To those who are most awake spiritually, this is an opportunity to participate fully in the cocreation of the life to follow. For most, however, the desire to take physical form once again is so compelling that any available option is taken. Unfortunately, in such circumstances, cocreative participation is ignored or neglected—particularly if the *bardo* experience was viewed as a chaotic or an out-of-control experience. For the less awakened, the physical gestation time may be perceived as an opportunity for a seeming much-needed rest from the *bardo* experience. In this case, it is likely spent in a state of stupor, wherein there is no availability to harvest the gems from the journey. Thus, one may be left with only the relative fear factor that was allocated to the experience.

For the one who is awake to the journey and to the distillation process following, however, the cocreative process is replete with possibilities. To the one thus awakened, an opportunity unfolds to ascertain the situation and circumstances wherein she might contribute the most goodness and wisdom in the life to follow. The awakened state also allows a kind of over-viewing that sees not only past energies that are leading up to the point in time one will be born but the potential outcomes of the creative forces in place from the perspective of any given point in time. In other words, this over-viewing is done from a perspective outside the boundaries of time and space, which opens the range of possibilities unimaginably.

Stay Awake!

The most important element in negotiating the creative journey from the point of death in one life to rebirth in the following life is staying awake. Even while having his students deep in meditation, the Buddha would loudly call out, "Wake up!" Clearly, this could prove a very startling experience to a meditator but was nonetheless effective. When the startle response is triggered, attention is single-pointed and intensified. This is the kind of attention the Buddha was trying to teach his disciples to apply *all the time*, since such is what provides the opportunity for seeing through the mind. Further, it is probably unrealistic to think one could hold that kind of single-pointed focus in the *bardo*, where appearances are so intense, if he has not mastered it in life.

Indeed, both the journey through a life and the journey through the *bardo* between lives exist to offer countless opportunities to awaken to the presence of essence, seeking to shine through the clouds of mind. The Buddha's call to awaken is pertinent to any state in which the mind finds itself, whether negotiating an apparent lifetime or an apparent *bardo* transit. Although many face the prospect of dying with tremendous fear, resistance and/or denial, there are salient reasons for approaching death with a unabashed curiosity. If one can remain awake and alert through the dying process and the journey that follows, an unprecedented opportunity opens to see and know what really is.

Just as one enters a perceived tunnel of profound light as one exits the body, so one has a near identical experience in the process of being born. As a new being enters and negotiates the birth canal, there is a point when the umbilicus is tightly pinched and the flow of oxygen to the baby is cut off. As oxygen is withheld from the brain, the optic nerves respond in a manner identical to the response noted above in the dying process. In other words, the infant sees a bright light as she is expelled from the birth canal. In a normal birth, the experience of "going into the light" is followed by the crowning of the head and the drawing out of the infant from the cramped quarters of the womb into what appears to be a vast spaciousness. Thus, in both entering and leaving a life, the journey is marked by profound light and exposure to unimaginable spaciousness—the true nature of everything.

There is one other human experience that is ushered in by the experience of profound light and boundless spaciousness—the dawning of one's enlightenment. As we have noted in our study, the realization of one's divine radiance is always available in every moment, whether at the moment of birth, in the journey of a life, at the moment of death or in the *bardo* transit. Indeed, the complex and poignant, if unconscious, physiological occurrences that provoke awareness of great light, marking both the entrance and exit points of each life, are set in place to prepare the evolving consciousness for the ultimate experience of light—the realization of enlightenment.

11

Where Is the Mind?

I t is interesting to note that while most people think they understand what the mind is, very few are capable of considering the
mind without seeing it in personal terms. This is interesting in
light of the fact that with every trip through the *bardo*, the "I" dissolves near the end of the journey as all reference points for that "I"
also dissolve. Since many people are inclined to believe that the
mind exists somewhere in the brain, they may also hold the notion
that just as the brain belongs to the designated self, so does the mind.
Yet in a vaster sense, there is really nothing to claim or own, since
the mind defies all faculties—even terminology—that would attempt
to lay hold to it.

The salient issue lies with the "I" (or the notion of "I") that regards
everything that arises in awareness to do so from either self or other.
This dualistic standard, however, cannot aptly apply to mind, for in
the truest sense, mind is nothing but a form of energy. Indeed, the
mind is a *field* of highly charged, aware energy, which can be extended
or moved by mere intention or curiosity. As such, there is no part of
mind for any "I" to own.

Exploring the Placement of Mind

Imagine for a moment yourself attending a concert—perhaps of a
celebrated violinist and piano accompanist. From your seat in the
audience, you pose the question, "Where is my mind?" Clearly some-

thing is there with you in your seat, looking out through your eyes, perhaps recognizing friends or acquaintances at the concert. When the concert begins, however, your focus of attention (or your mind) moves to the musicians, and you could say its field has been extended to the performers and the performance. If you happen to know the musical piece that is being played, your expectation of what is coming next musically speaking has moved your mind into the future as well.

Then further imagine that as you are listening at a particularly poignant musical moment, someone behind you sneezes, interrupting both your attention and the smooth flow you are enjoying of the music. Your mind field is extended, through the startle of interruption, to the person behind you. However, it is also taking in information from all the others in the audience who were startled by the sneeze, still following the expectation of the flow of the music, in addition to observing whether or not the interruption disturbed the concentration of the musicians. So where is the mind?

Assume for a moment, to further explore the placement of mind, that the concert you are attending is being filmed to air on TV the following night. Move your imaginative activity now to the following evening, and see yourself at home enjoying the concert once again, but this time in a televised presentation. As you view yourself watching the television broadcast, see a young child with you who has never before seen a television. As you listen to the recorded concert and view the child, it becomes clear to you that the child believes the musicians are actually playing from within the television box. She has no understanding of how a television broadcast is generated, and thus to her the musicians are in that box, happily playing their music!

Here let us return to our earlier question: "Where is the mind?" If you are one who holds that the mind is located within the brain, perhaps an analogy can be drawn to the child mentioned in the paragraph above. Indeed, believing that the mind is in the brain is tantamount to the child's belief that the performers she viewed on television were *in* the TV set. As an adult who has knowledge of TV broadcasting, however, you know that the music performance was coming to you *through* the TV—it being but a receiver set that interrupts the energy patterns that are broadcast from a source many miles away.

As waves of energy (the broadcast frequencies) are received by a TV set, they are then translated into electrical impulses that produce images on the screen. Because of your familiarity with television, you know that the set is the receiver, not the broadcaster, of the programs you watch. Unlike the child, you would not think the TV set is the creator of the programs. The same is true of your brain: It is a receiver set, receiving the perceptions the mind broadcasts.

The mind is an aware field of energy that moves in the direction of attention, curiosity and/or intention. It both intercepts and may be intercepted by other fields of aware energy. For example, when you pray for someone or send your intentions for healing to someone, you actually extend your field of awareness to them and your field intercepts their field, often creating powerful—even palpable—experiences. However, it cannot be said that this experience is happening in the brain. *Where* it happens is somewhere in the two intersecting fields of awareness. When one field of awareness extends itself into another field of awareness, particularly in the ways referenced above, there also arises an opportunity for dissolution of the "I."

Mind Awareness after Death

Another, albeit somewhat different, example of fields of awareness extending and intersecting is what has been termed communication with the dead. In these situations, it becomes quite clear that one's awareness continues not only along his or her personal path, continuing to interface with the fields of awareness of other still embodied, but can also interface with the fields of awareness of those (or some) who are no longer in physical embodiment. Although such might seem a natural phenomenon around the time someone actually dies or shortly thereafter, it may not seem so natural at a distance in the future. Yet there are numerous examples of situations where communication between a living person and one who has died has gone on for years—even *after* the time for the departed loved one to have taken rebirth. Clearly, such experiences go significantly beyond the "normal" experience but do substantiate that mind continues even after the brain is dead and rotting.

This is an area into which analytical mind has difficulty entering. Contemplative mind, even if it does not fully understand the process, is much more useful here. After one exits a particular life, unless one attains enlightenment in that life, there is a designated "package" of energy that retains its relative configuration. This package of energy has the ability (or energetic force) to reflect the personality, history, developmental process and wisdom of the life just past, and can both extend itself into and be extended into by other fields of awareness.

If in a given life an individual was well-known, that energy package can retain its configuration for literally hundreds of years. There are numerous people (mostly American, as in the cases below) who have meaningful and substantive conversations with such great people as Albert Einstein, Abraham Lincoln, Thomas Jefferson, Benjamin Franklin, Henry Ford and others for whom they nurture profound respect. How is this possible in light of the fact that all these have surely gone on to other lives since their appearance in American history?

Try to hold in mind here that even though a given individual's body form expired, the work they came to accomplish may not necessarily have been completed. Further, in the cases of great ones such as those named above, generally they are not simply single individuals taking embodiment who happen to fall into greatness. Rather, they are often the result of a kind of "group project," where numerous flows of light—which might be understood as a group of soul extensions—converge along their highest frequencies to precipitate a path along which a great being may arise.

In truth, all of humanity interfacing with the planet at the time of a great one has some part in the raising of that one. Such is nothing but a merging of massive fields of consciousness extending together into an expression of Oneness. Often, however, even after having made the contributions of a life that rises to fame throughout the world, the body may expire even though the instructional potential continues through time. For this reason, something must exist to allow such to continue—without a body.

Granted, these are complicated matters, matters that stretch the generally accepted boundaries of logic and understanding. Fortunately, those assumed boundaries are collective projections and have no more innate "reality" than any other projection. As should be seen at this point of our text, simplistic terminology cannot approach the profound miracle of consciousness, for such is the Source of All Being extending Itself through all levels of sentient awareness and in infinite applications, all reflecting Itself *to Itself*. Whether we speak of mind, awareness, consciousness or the Light of the Infinite, we speak of the same thing—just different applications and potential applications.

Facing the *Bardo*

In the *bardo*, the mind (and its "I"-ness) is unraveled by the continual manifestation of karmic projections. Technically speaking, the mind is the container for awareness. Thus, when the container dissolves, awareness is released in somewhat the same fashion that the mind is released from its anchoring point in the physical body at the point of death. In each case, a rapid expansion takes place that demonstrates something about the true nature of awareness—hopefully, at profounder and profounder levels as one cycles through many lifetimes and *bardo* experiences. When awareness is released from the confines of mind, numerous potentials arise, one being that of extension into the infinite flow of radiant energy (call it love) that is both beginningless and endless. Indeed, such is the divine function of awareness.

Awareness at all levels—even at the most condensed or constricted levels—is continually being prompted to greater expansion. While limited by a body-mind (perhaps one with an impermeable sense of "I"), this natural expansion is confined, or trapped. However, when consciousness is freed from the confines of body and of mind, the potential for unification with the Infinite is at its highest probability.

For many, the thought of facing the *bardo* seems frightening, perhaps too intense to bear. Indeed, some of the experiences of the journey do in fact generate tremendous intensity. Yet the potential to slip into the natural state, merged with the divine, is unequaled in body-mind life experiences. That being said, it also remains true that most individuals who actualize their enlightenment do so while in physical form. To the awakened *bardo* traveler, it is the very experience of the *bardo* that often propels one into a life in which one finds profound awakening, or self-realization. Simply stated, there is no experience in the body-mind state that reveals the true nature of mind so profoundly as does the *bardo* journey.

As the mind unravels, streams of light—*aware* light—are revealed to the one who is awake enough to recognize it. These streams of light are emitted by the Infinite through one's liberated mind when karmic projections are transcended or dissolved. These streams of aware light are encoded with the formula, not only for personal enlightenment, but for planetary enlightenment as well. Indeed, such is the formula for Creation of this cosmic experience. Thus, hidden within those *bardo* experiences that seem so frightening is direct access to the mathematical explanation or formula for the transformation that all seek— indeed, the transformation that the entire cosmos seeks!

The formula is not understandable to the linear, or analytical, mind. However, when awareness released from the mind encounters this formula within the streaming love of the Infinite, a rapid expansion occurs, releasing the infinite light of consciousness from awareness. As can be seen, this creative pattern evolves along a divine continuum. As mind is released from the body container at the point of death, as awareness is released from the container of mind in the *bardo*, so infinite light is released from the container of awareness in a flash of exuberant union with the cosmos.

If one is caught in the stupor of fear, however, or asleep in the trance of karmic projections, the *bardo* journey may prove to be more an experience of "endarkenment" rather than one of enlightenment. Perhaps it is an unconscious memory from previous *bardo* journeys that accounts for the fact that so many people fear death. Within the creative core there may exist a reservoir of frightening experiences that, although lost to conscious memory, still generate a strong influence on the psyche. Further, in cultures where there is no real training for the in-between state—or perhaps a categorical denial of future lives—the content of the "forgotten memory" may arise as one nears death or perhaps watches a loved one die. Thus, the process of transition may be further complicated by these specific projections based on past experience.

Learn to Tame the Mind

The best advice a teacher can give an aspirant regarding living, dying and becoming enlightened is to tame the mind. What could be more important than learning to cut through the mind's projections? As has been noted in earlier chapters, viable mind training requires developing specific skills: concentration and strong focus; challenging projections as they arise in the mind; cultivating the qualities of enlightened mind; and moving with the call of heightened awareness to continually expand.

To the extent possible, it is useful to draw parallels between the experiences herein described in realms beyond the scope of physicality and experiences one undergoes in daily life. This practice is helpful since it is preparatory work for when one actually enters the *bardo*. Just contemplating the *bardo* is helpful as well, for it provides the continuity from life to death that may be missing in ordinary circumstances, particularly in the West.

In addition to the practices above, there is yet one other that has proven useful in negotiating the *bardo* with the goal of enlightenment—that of working directly with the formula for enlightenment. Few have stumbled upon it without a preceding heightened *bardo* experience, since full comprehension of the formula cannot be contained by or placed within the normal configuration of mind. Since planetary enlightenment is the goal of the Aquarian Age, the movement into this New Age opens both individual and collective experiences of psyche to profound new realizational levels. This is a time when humanity must rise to new levels of trustworthiness and responsibility in order to use well the potential openings in consciousness that are becoming available. As they become available, mind must dissolve into consciousness, for mind is too small a container for the expansive provision of beingness that is possible for unfettered consciousness: union with the divine.

The practice referred to above is that of contemplating and meditating upon the formula for enlightenment. Clearly, this formula should not be approached as some cosmic secret available only to some chosen few. Rather, it should be approached as a tremendously powerful spiritual realization, available to all who can come to understand it—or at least open to it. As the critical mass of the planet is approached, shifts in consciousness become possible that were not previously possible due to the force exerted on the old paradigm by the consciousness expanding. While this same force can produce considerable chaos in the world, the chaos—like those encounters in the *bardo*—may be hiding something rare, wonderful and utterly transcendent.

Be the Radiant Glory You Were Meant to Be

As mind dissolves into consciousness, revealing the true nature of everything to all who find union with beingness, many revelations are likely to emerge in the field of awareness that creates, supports, sustains and ultimately reclaims each piece of consciousness formerly confined by mind. It is unto this radiant glory that all efforts to break the bonds of suffering are dedicated. As the profound coalescing of light generates a great awakening among the minds of humanity, may each and every designated being of light receive and give forth the brilliant radiance it was meant to reflect. May truth be unequivocally established in the life stream of Earth!

To the discovery of the profound within the mundane, the infinite within the finite, the sacred within the profane, the formula for enlightenment is hereby offered for the liberation of all sentient beings. May all beings everywhere receive countless blessings with the encounter of this great mystery: $1 + 1 = 0$.